100 Crappy Drawings

Jan-Hein Arens

Broadway Disasters Publishing

Table of contents

Text & drawings: Jan-Hein Arens
Editor: Rogier Weenen

Design: Broadway Disasters Publishing
Distribution: Brave New Books

ISBN: 9789402101102

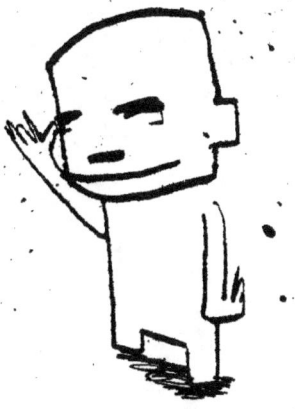

Why publish a book?

A couple of years ago, in 2008, I got a call from a lady with a heavy French accent. At first I thought it was a joke but it turned out she was actually French, and was working for gallery Carré d'Artistes. The concept of the gallery was quite simple; just make 40 drawings and send them by mail. The gallery would put them on display, and if some work was sold I would get an order to make new drawings. Up until that time the only reason for me to draw was when I ran out of money to buy paint or canvases. I didn't think they would sell anything, and that the French did not have a sense of humor, but decided to give it a try anyway. Drawing was a good practice, and it would look great on my resume to mention a foreign gallery.

Now, five years later, I have delivered and sold more than 250 drawings and they have travelled around the world. Also I discovered that drawing is an art form that suits me more than fine. It's nothing fancy, just a piece of paper, a bit of paint, some blue and white drawing chalk, and pen and ink. But opposed to painting it is very fast, and I like fast. I even have a hairdryer in my studio to dry paint so I can move on (also lots of coffee and loud music help).

Enough with the artistic romance, let's get on to the drawings. In this book you find a selection of 100 drawings, sold in different galleries over the years. I redid them, because the originals were in color. If a single drawing is framed, color is great, but once they are made into a book it will look more like a candy store than an art book. And yes, I did take the opportunity to correct and improve some.

Have fun;

Jan-Hein Arens

Part 1

About you and me and everything
in between.

1. I will lie down, and
   pretend to be dead (fig.1)

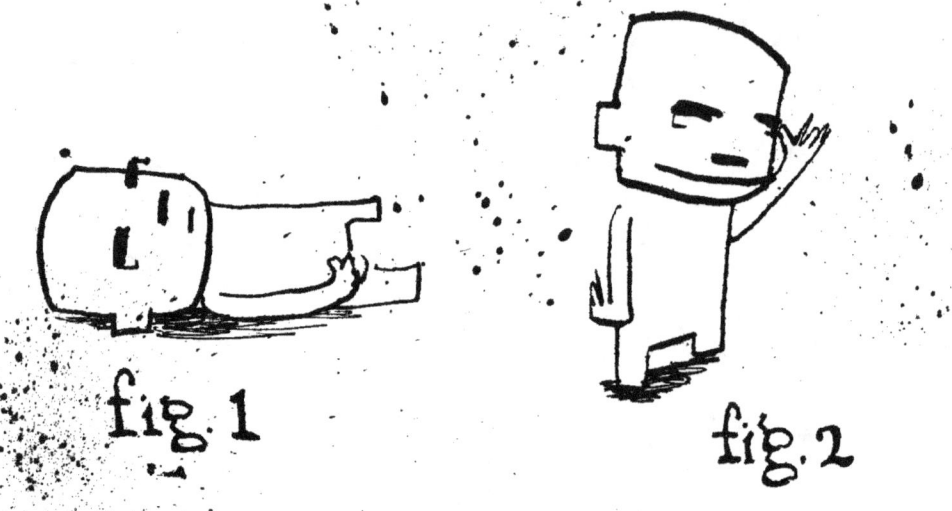

fig.1   fig.2

2. When everybody is all sad and stuff
   I will get up and pretend to be alive. (fig.2)

At night the bats came to warn me.

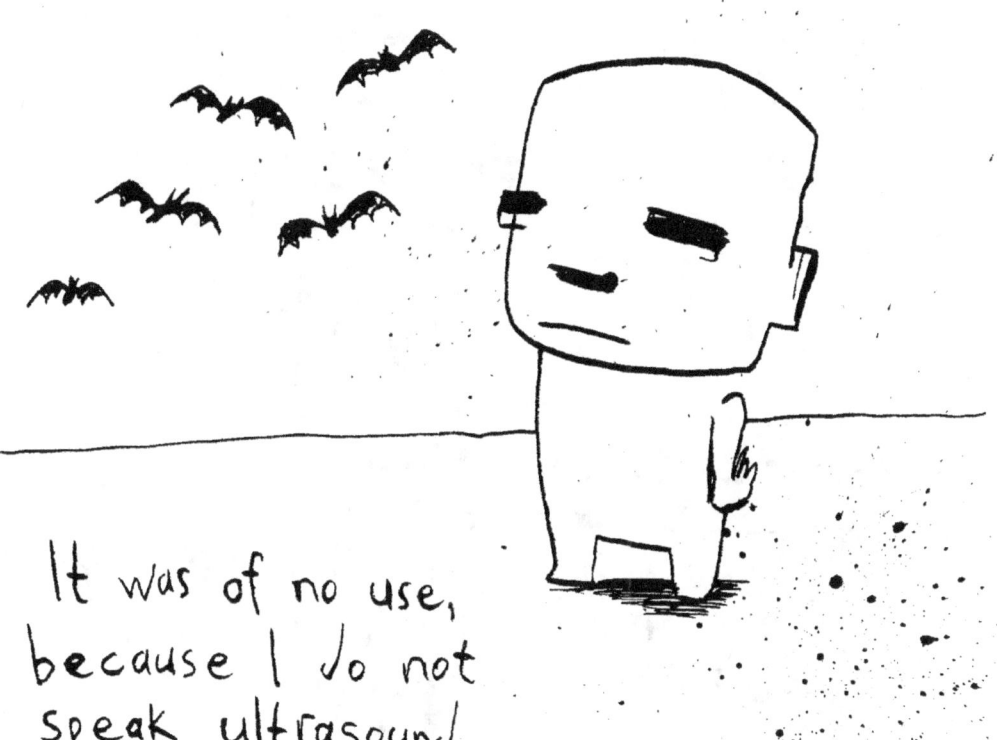

It was of no use, because I do not speak ultrasound.

I stared at the plate for 40 days and 40 nights.

Now I am quite hungry

Good deeds that go unnoticed:

Sometimes I dress up like a bullet,

hide myself in the closet,

and kill <u>no</u> one!

I once build a giant castle.

but then I tore it down

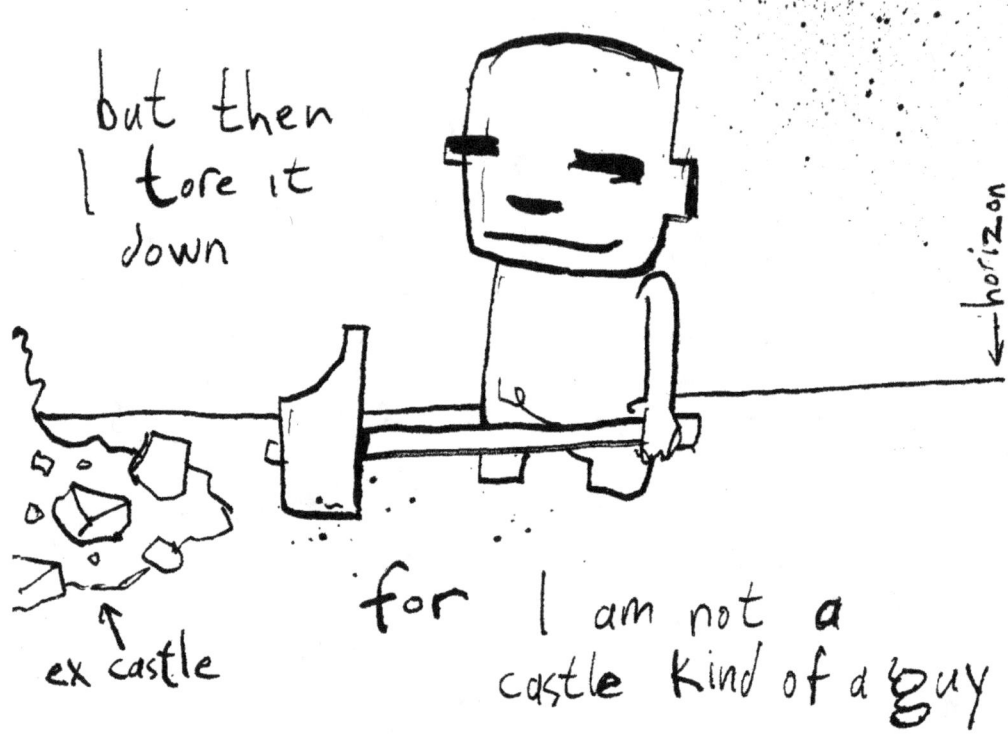

← horizon

ex castle

for I am not a castle kind of a guy

Connect the dots

you

1 •

2 •

reality

I took some slight imperfections,

and turned them into a full-blown disaster.

Enjoy now, thank me later.

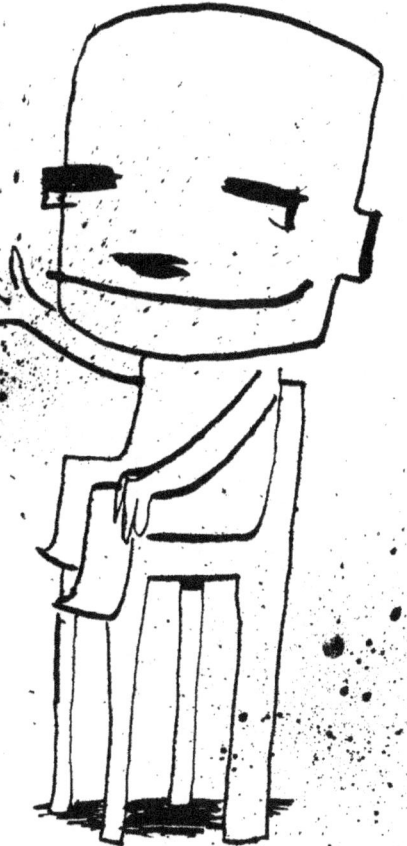

When you leave,
we dance.

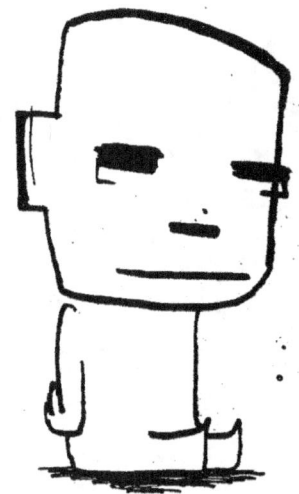
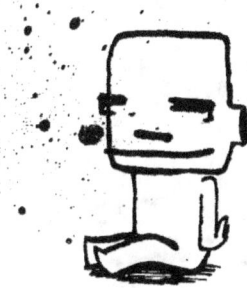

When you return,
we pretend nothing happened.

I used to be a child,

horizon →

Hidden diseases
part 2: childhood

but then I
got better.

For you;

I will scream,
I will shout,
I will sell drugs
to small children!

← horizon

I just wanted
a hug,
but she told me
to do the dishes first.

Now she won't
hug me, because
my hands are all wet.

Damn you,
Dishes!

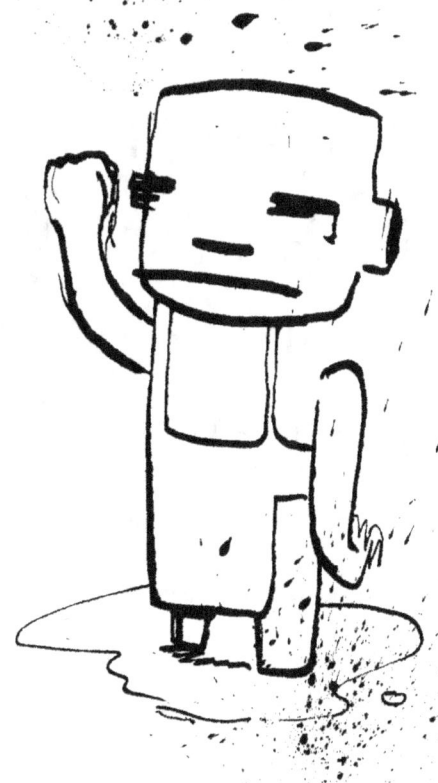

My kids can't believe
I am making money with these
crappy drawings

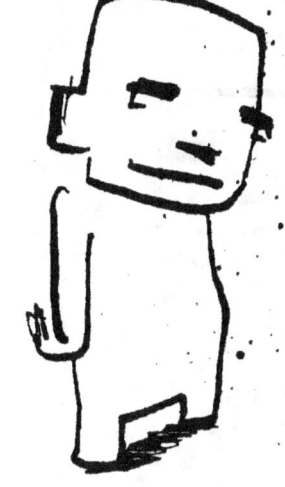
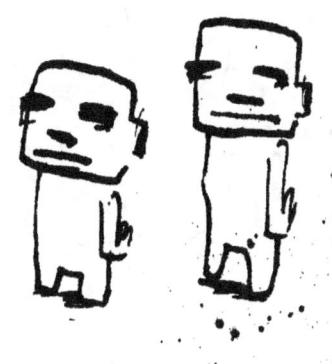

neither can I

Helmet

I always wear
a helmet.

If some one tries
to swallow me,
he'll choke.

shadow

Her life is a joke

and I am the punch line

This diagram is to explain some things:

Society   me   Secret Society.

Spider

Here I stand,

In a
monumental
kind of way.

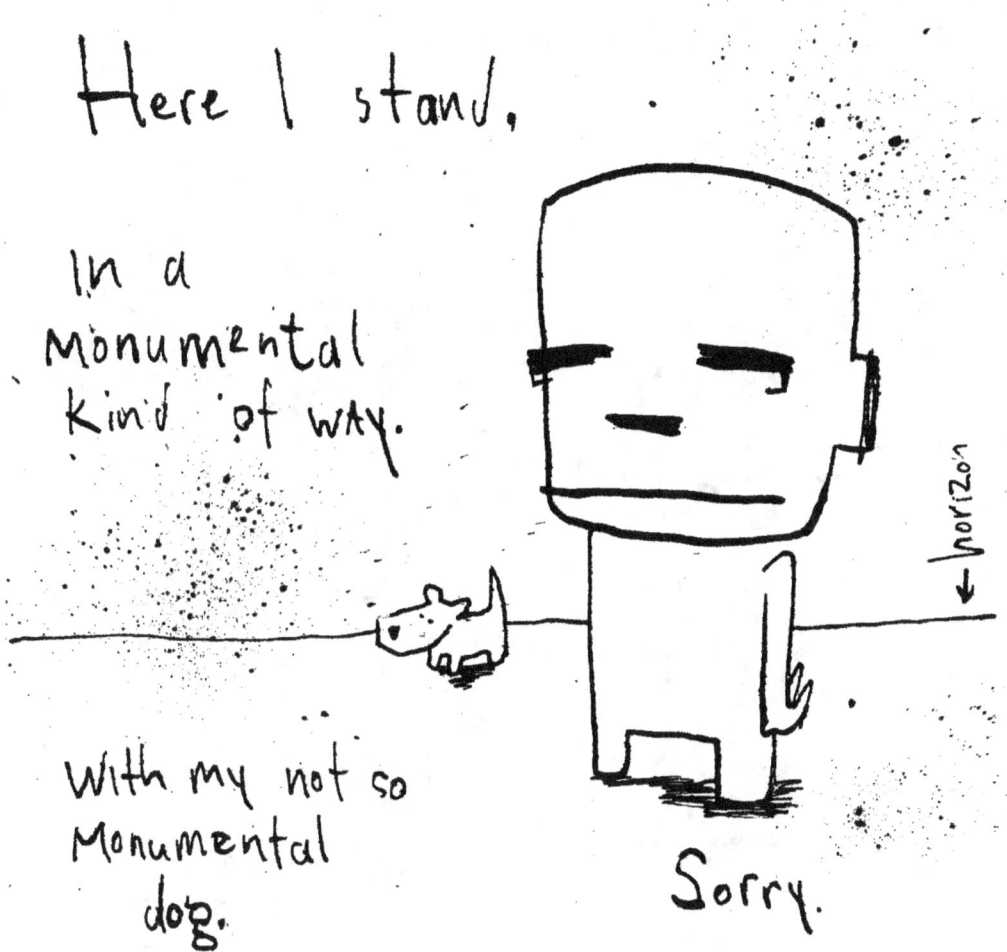

← horizon

With my not so
Monumental
dog.

Sorry.

"211, 877, 593, 11, 947"
was what the horse
whispered softly in
my ear.

But I couldn't
care less.

I don't even
like prime numbers.

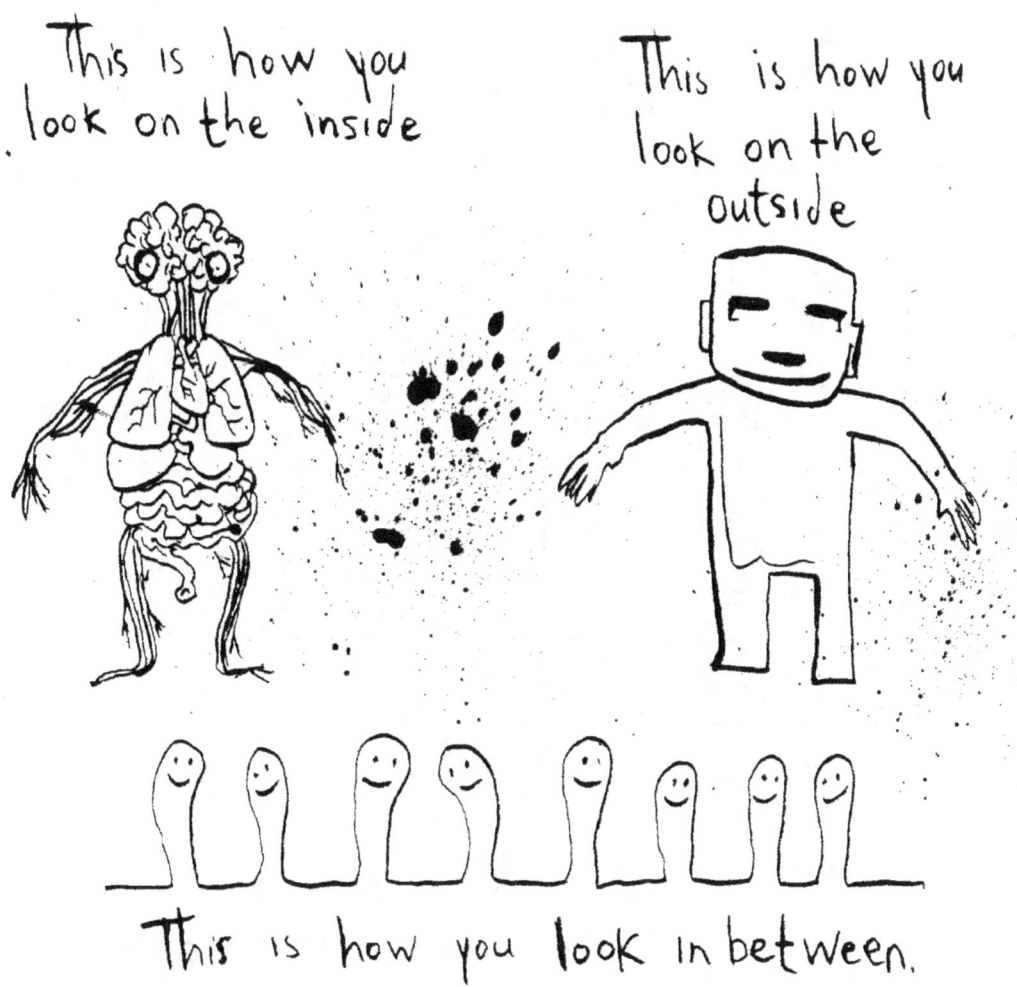

My job

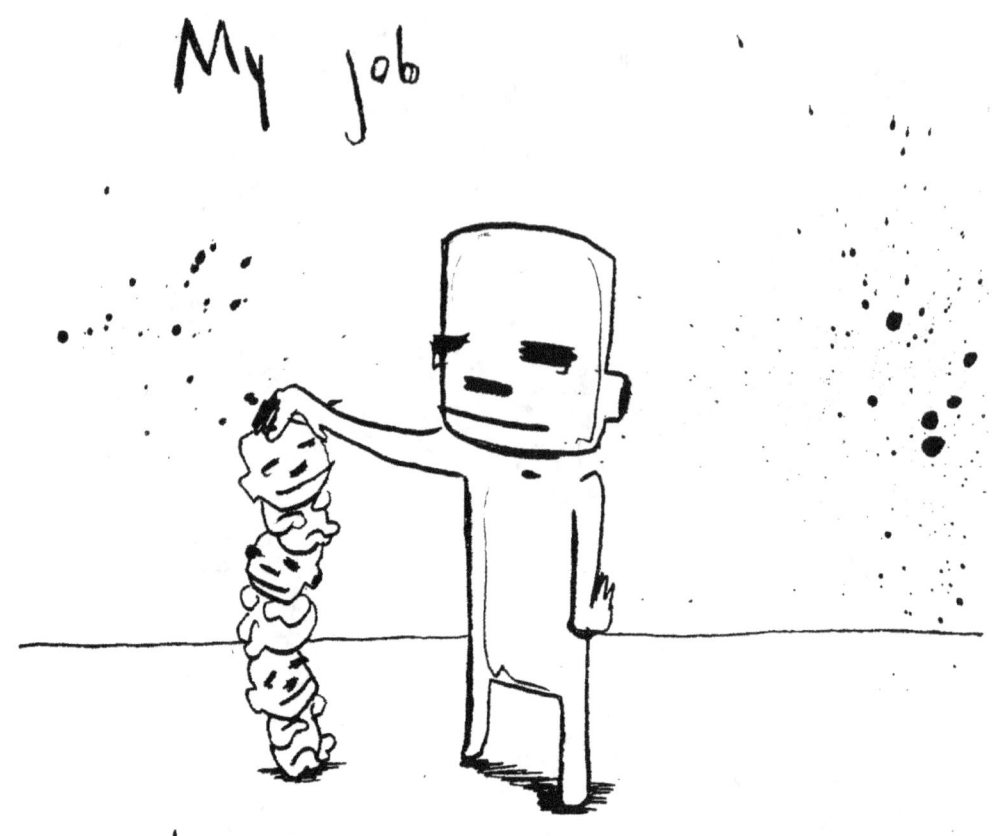

it is my job to make sure
this pile of babies does not collapse.

My thoughts
are like the
branches of a
tree

they grow
without ever
touching
something solid

This is Nathan.

He will replace you when you are dead.

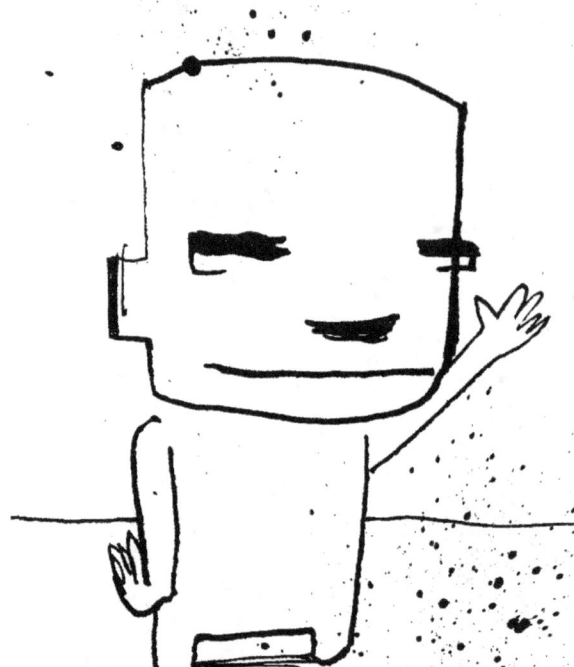

But for now he just needs to use your bathroom.

I used to be an awesome Ninja

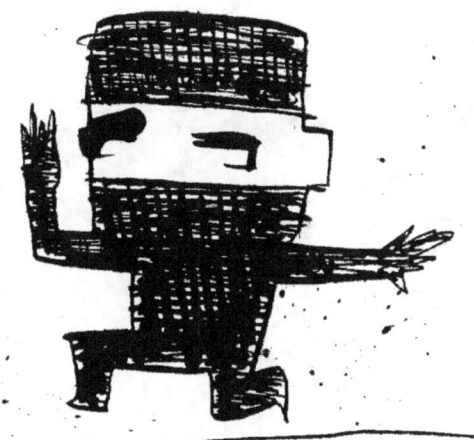

awesome Ninja

← horizon

←shadow

Now I am just a Ninja

Save my soul, and it will be yours for ever and ever*

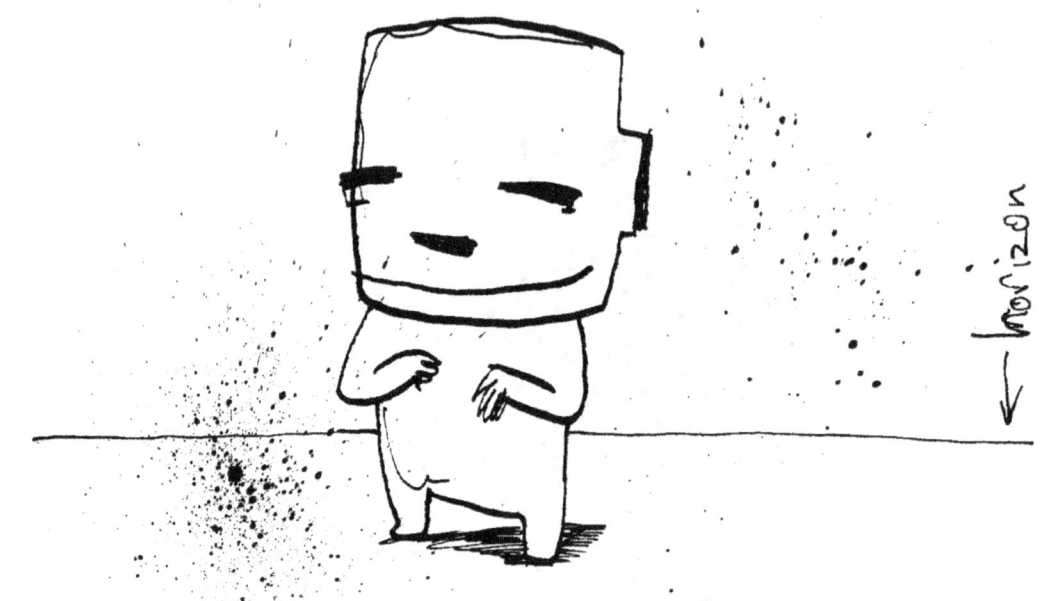

horizon

*= except for tuesdays, then it's my moms

I am ready for
everything!

except spiders

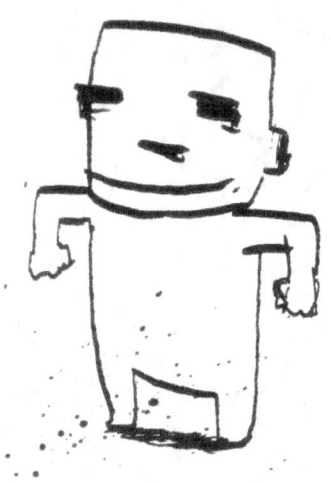

God, I hate
spiders!

First I will write the book

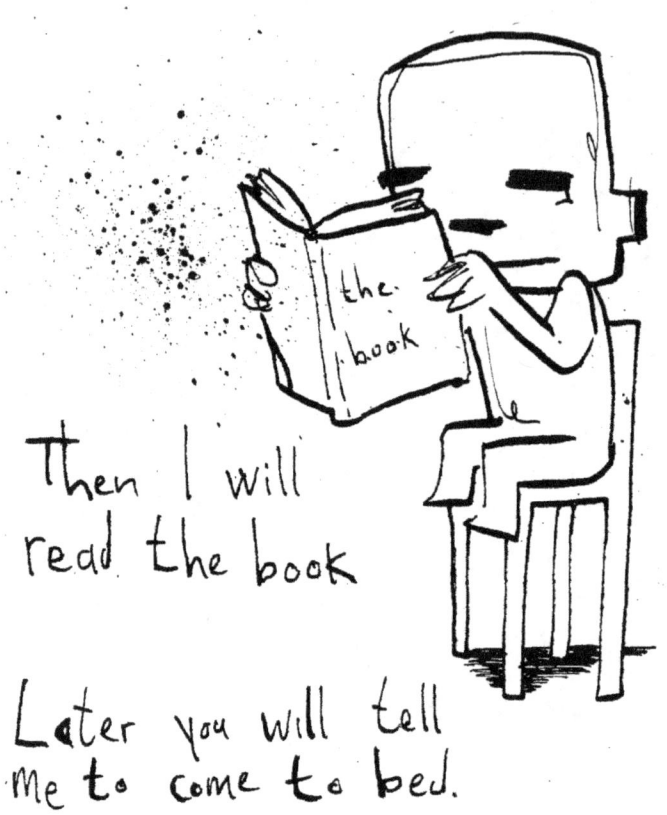

Then I will read the book

Later you will tell me to come to bed.

This is me,

thinking about
things that
matter.*

* like food or video games

I practiced and practiced

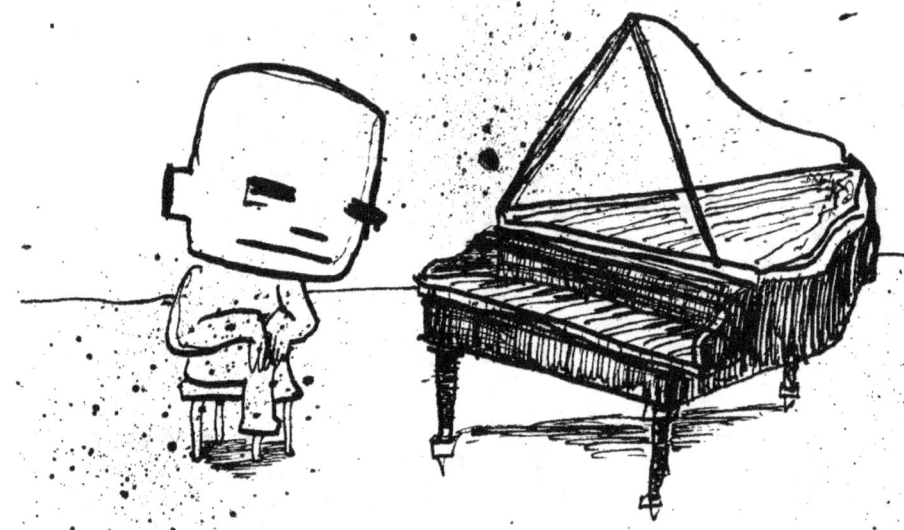

But still I could not think
like a Piano.

This kid will end up
just like you.

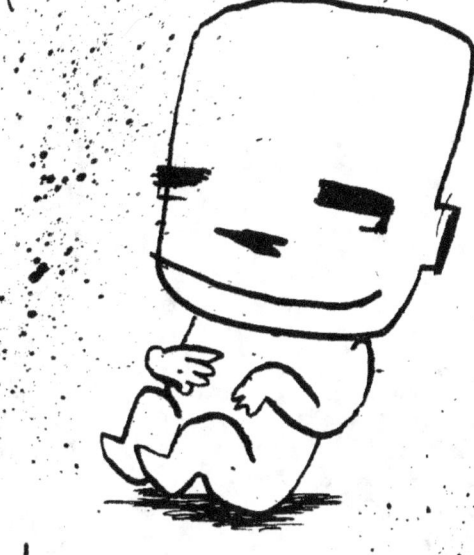

So, for god's sake,
do something stupid.

I ♥ tiny nuclear explosions

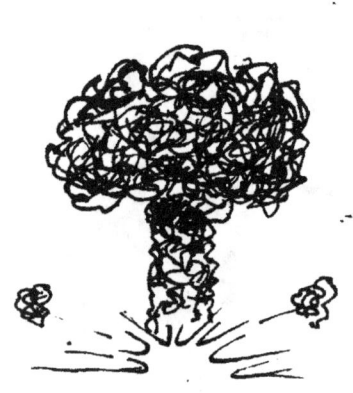

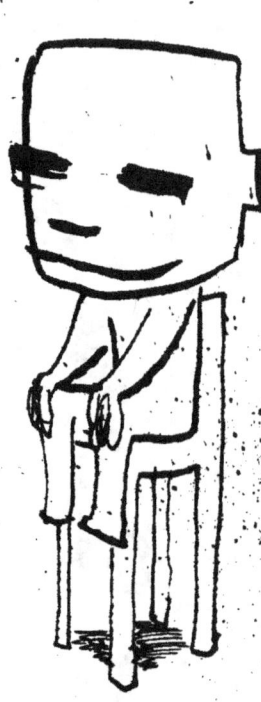

I do not understand this music.

I think it is
because the
composer does
not understand me.

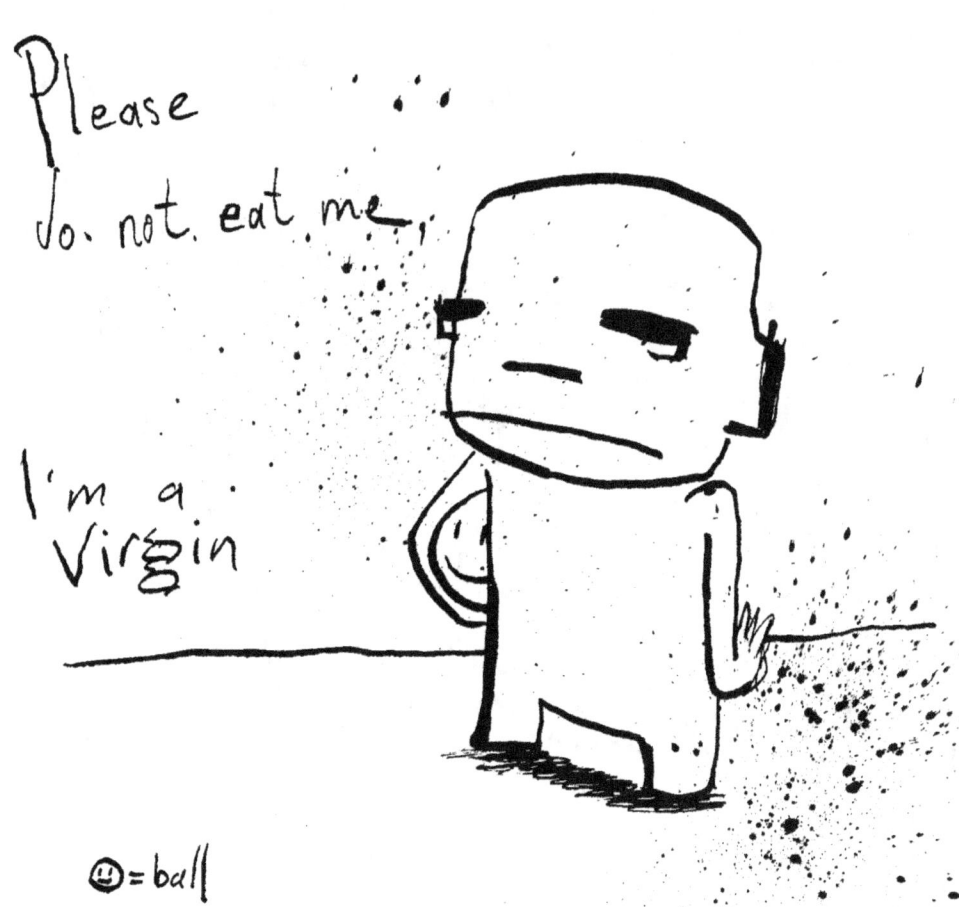

The great wall of truth
is about to come down.

And I am ready to hide
in the debris.

I want you
to want me

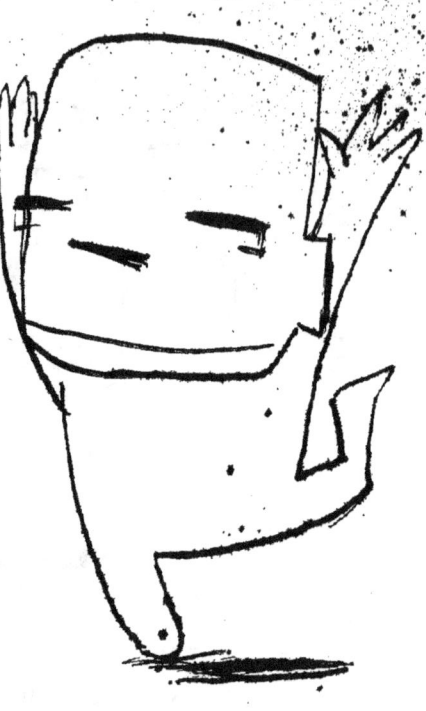

In an abstract
kind of way (or
conceptual).

What happened?

☐ You traveled through time and space in a nonlinear way

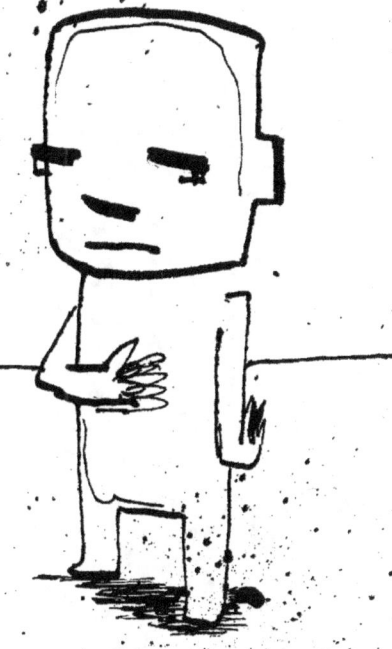

☐ You should not have eaten that tuna sandwich

Part 2

About God, love and other things that help you sleep at night.

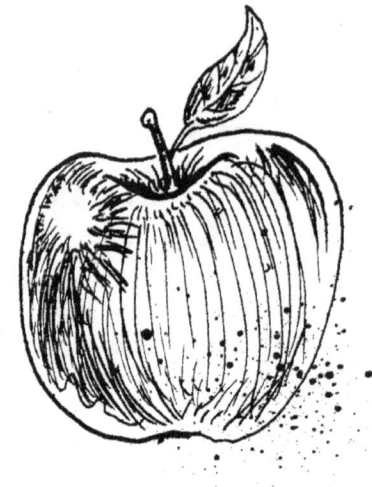

Sometimes I think god is an apple.

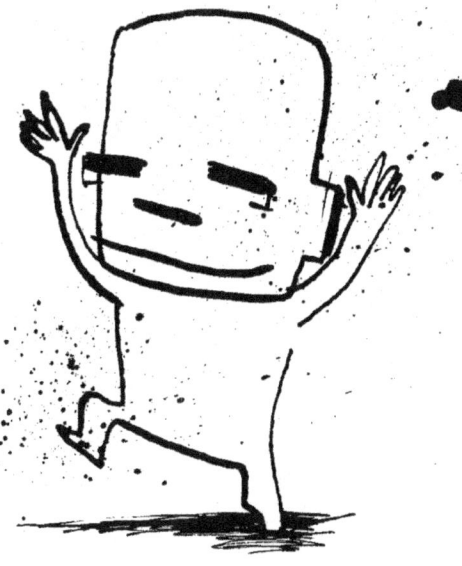

But most of the times I don't think at all.

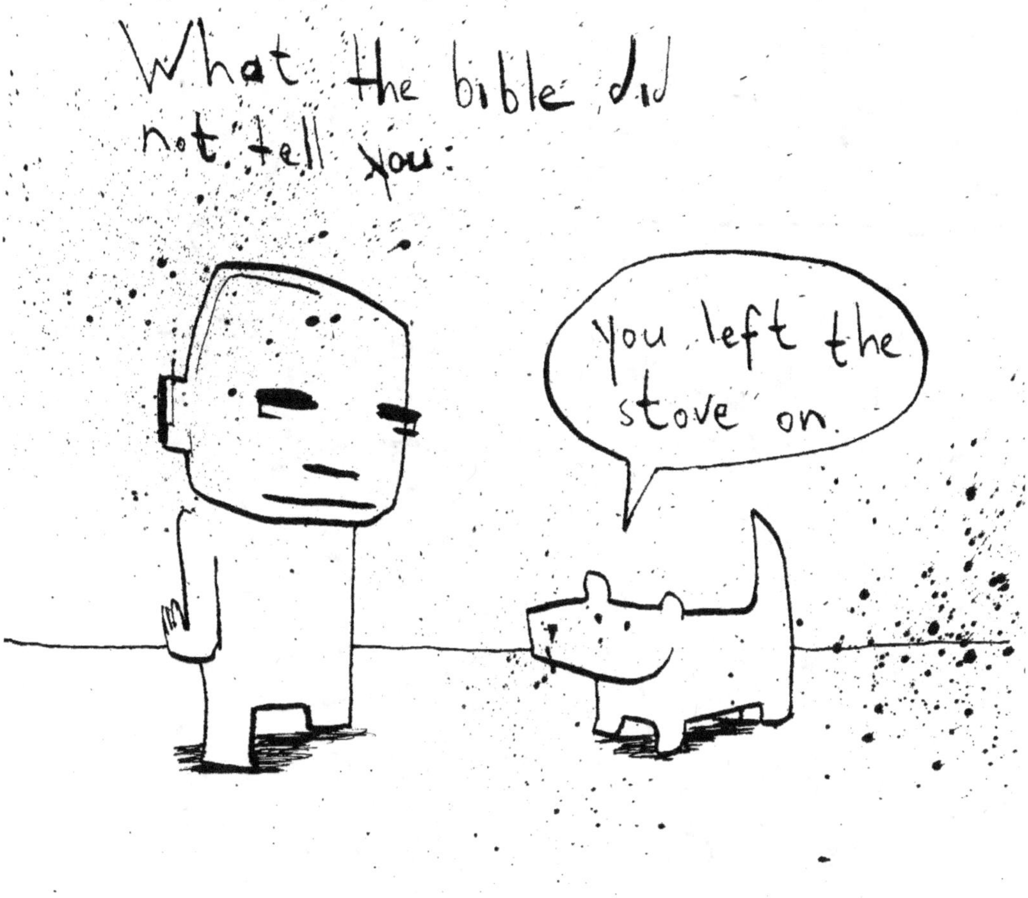
What the bible did not tell you:
you left the stove on.

Clouds

Never trust
anything that
floats

How to crossover from the dark side:

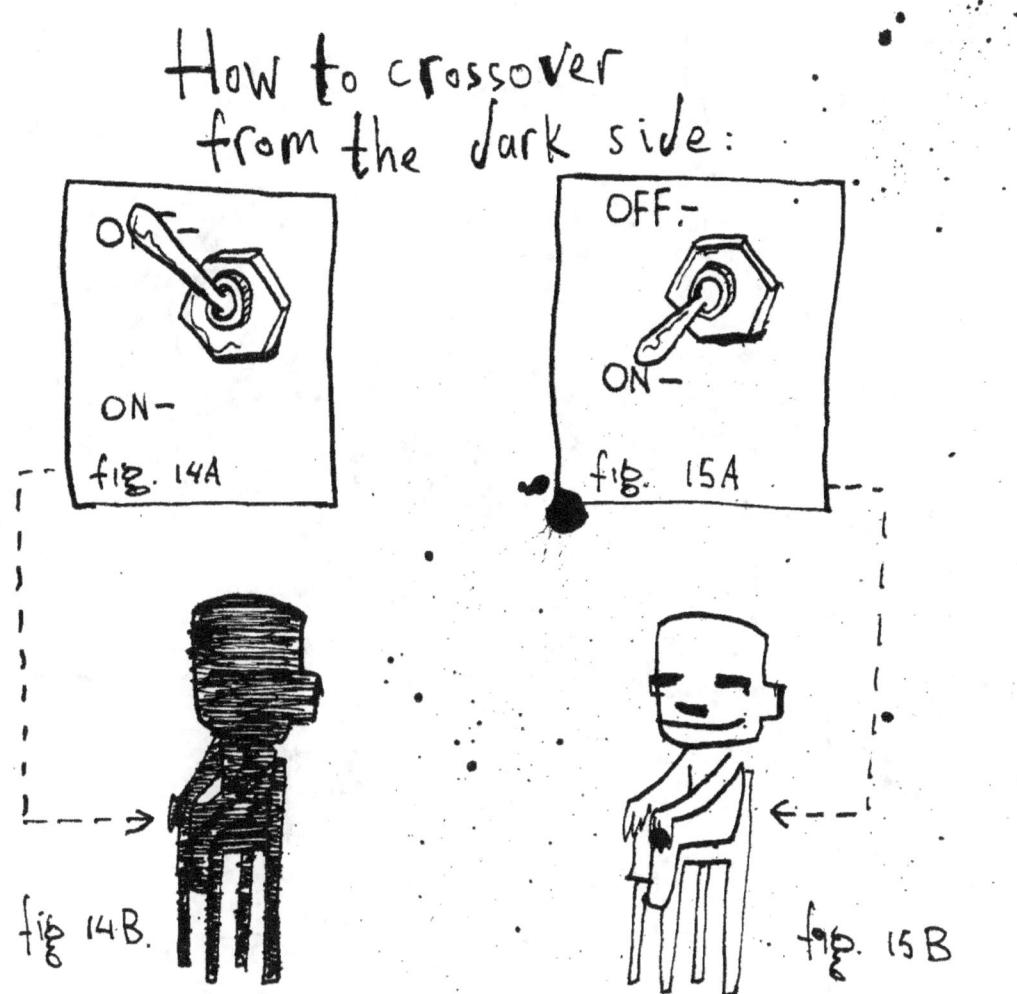

ON—

ON—

fig. 14A

OFF.—

ON—

fig. 15A

fig 14B.

fig. 15 B

Hidden diseases part 1..
Telepathy

It's a handicap,
not a lifestyle!

All of a sudden
the fish tank disappeared.

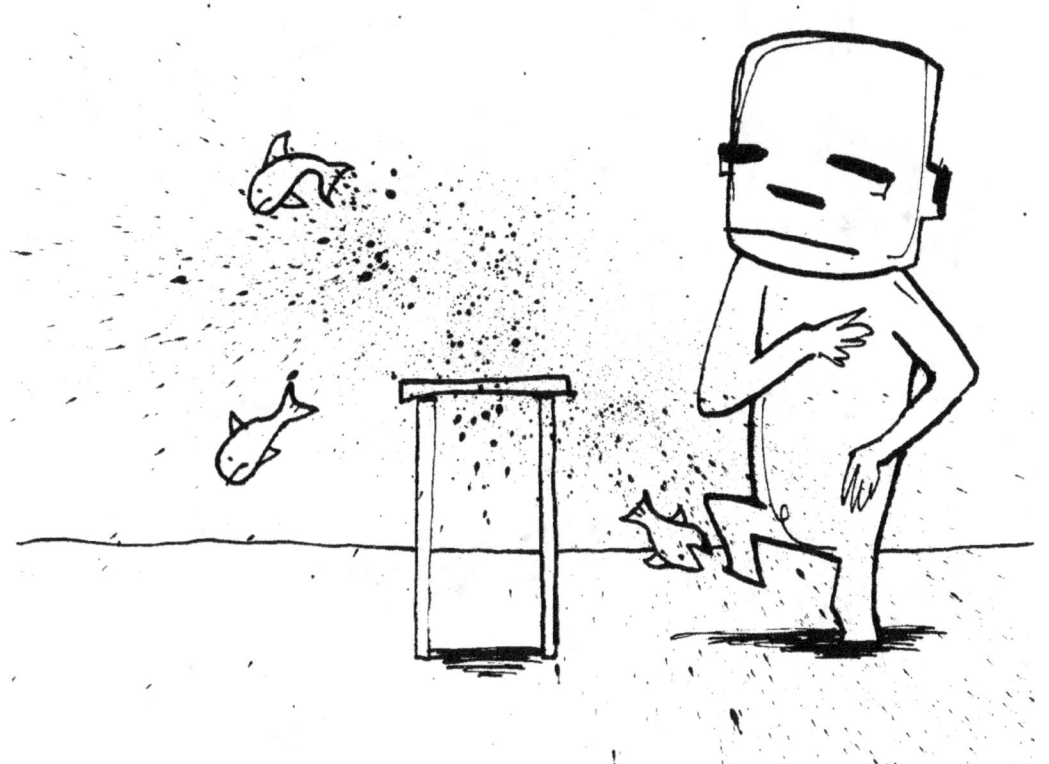

The angel said:

Go ahead,
It's OK to
eat the cake.

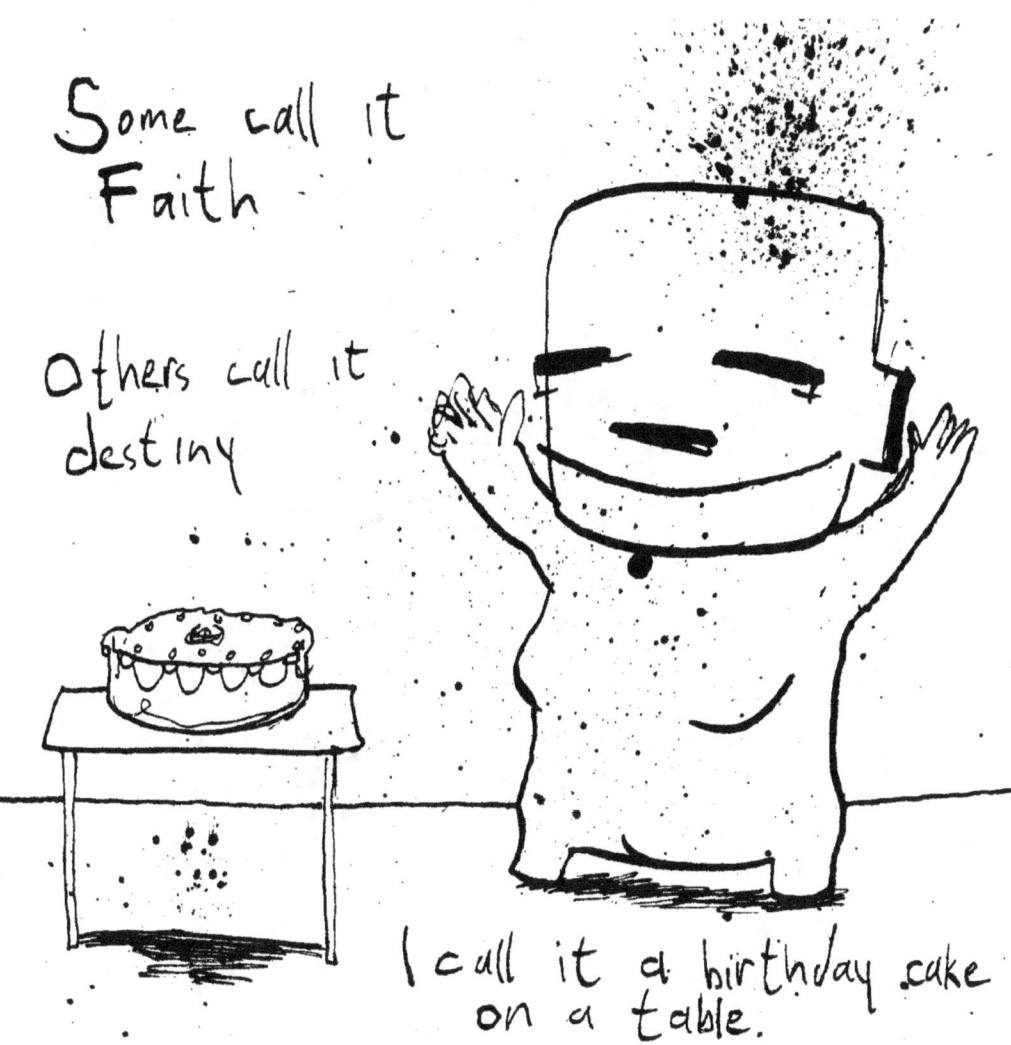

Some call it Faith

Others call it destiny

I call it a birthday cake on a table.

god lives
in my Fishtank

Impending Doom

God told me to lose my keys, so I did.

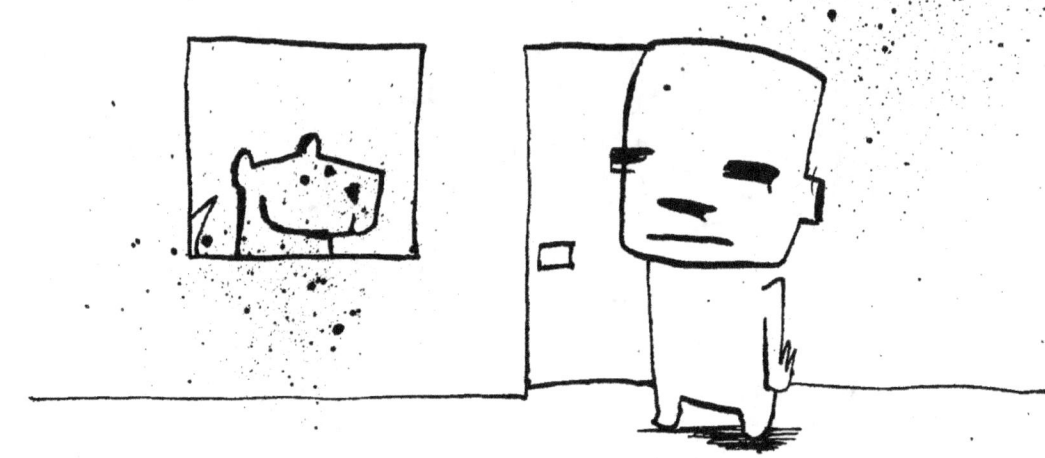

Now I wish god will tell the dog to open the door.

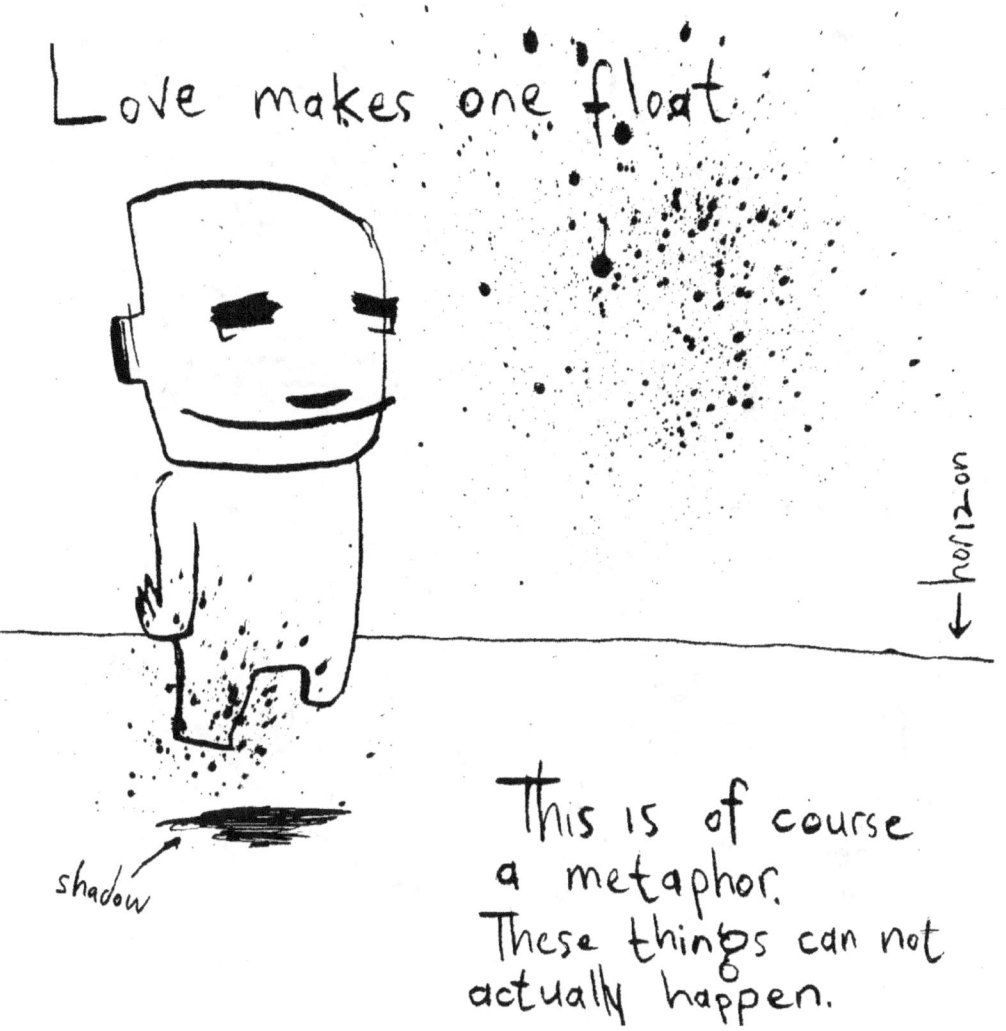

Love makes one float

shadow

horizon →

This is of course
a metaphor.
These things can not
actually happen.

The great machine of love

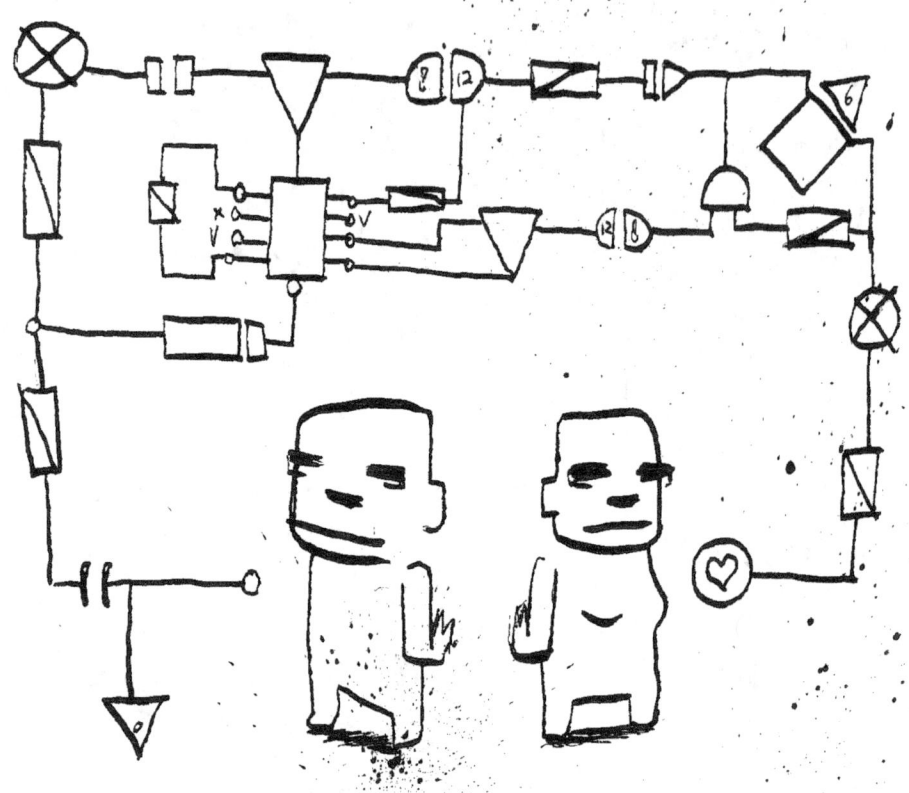

Even as a child
Satan was quite
evil.

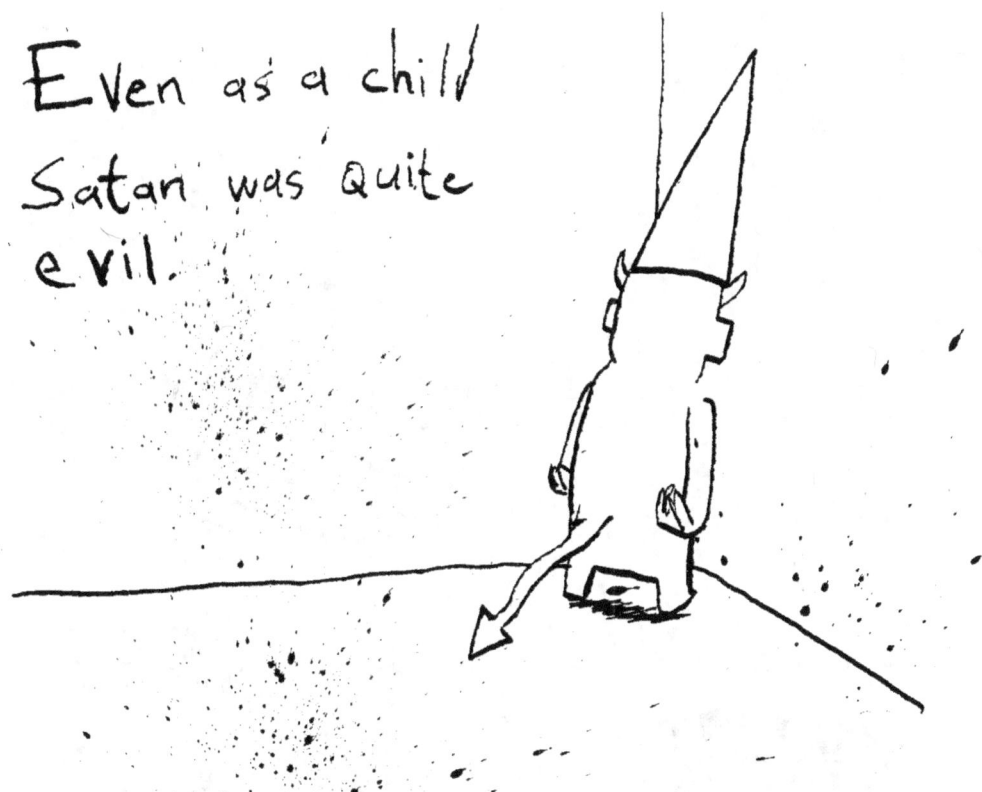

Sea of love

horizon

turned into a
puddle of joy.

An angel appeared, and he told
us about the benefits of
being self-employed

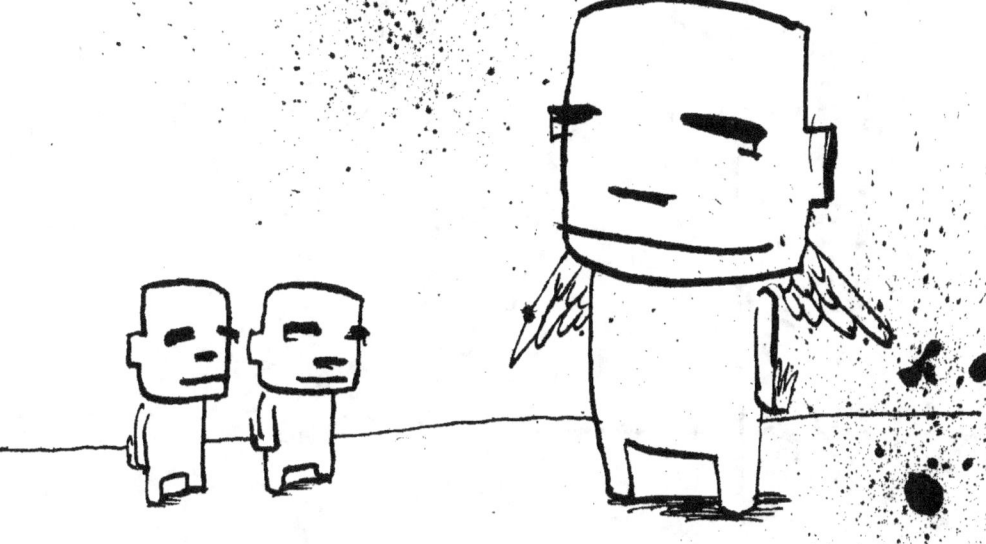

The next day we opened a
sandwich shop, and lived
average ever after

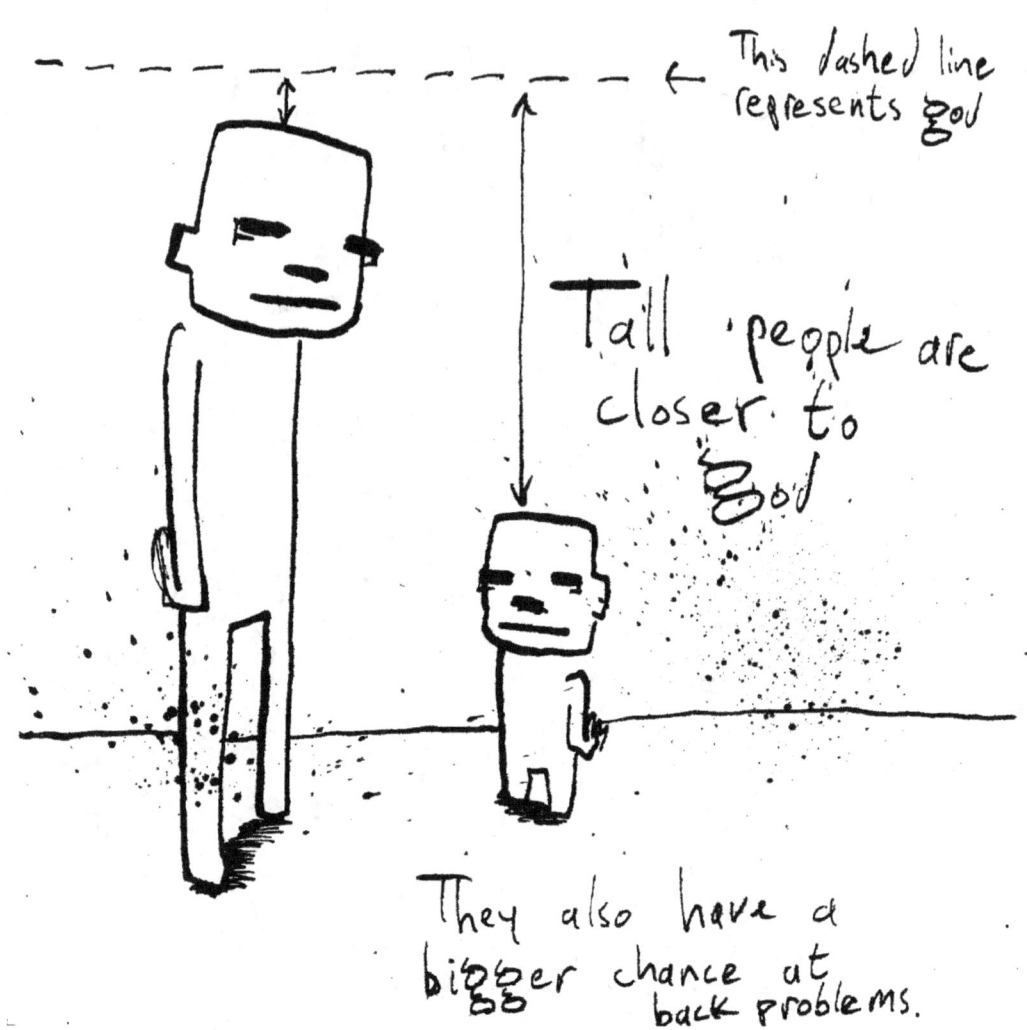

This dashed line represents god

Tall people are closer to god

They also have a bigger chance at back problems.

God was too busy to forgive me

So he sent me
a letter telling
me not to worry
so much.

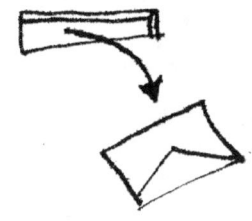

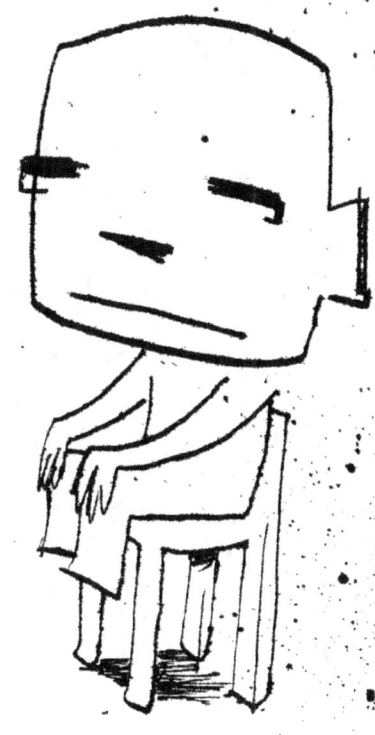

To live is to doubt.

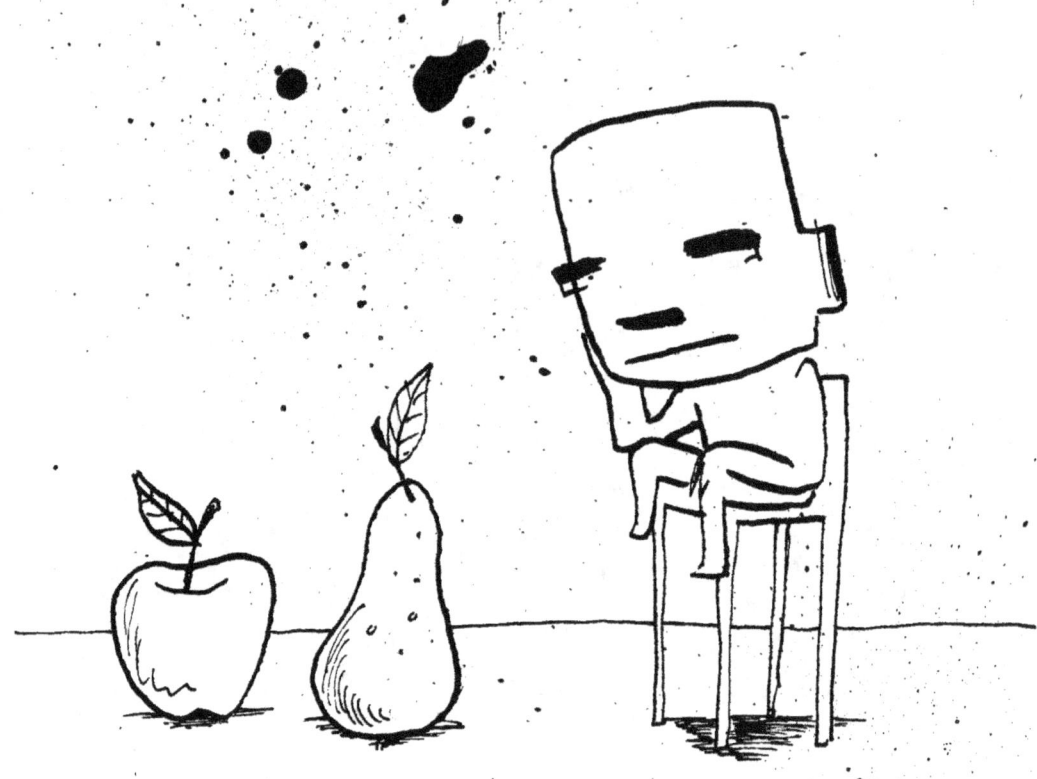

Love
~~Art~~
What is it for
and why should we
care about it?

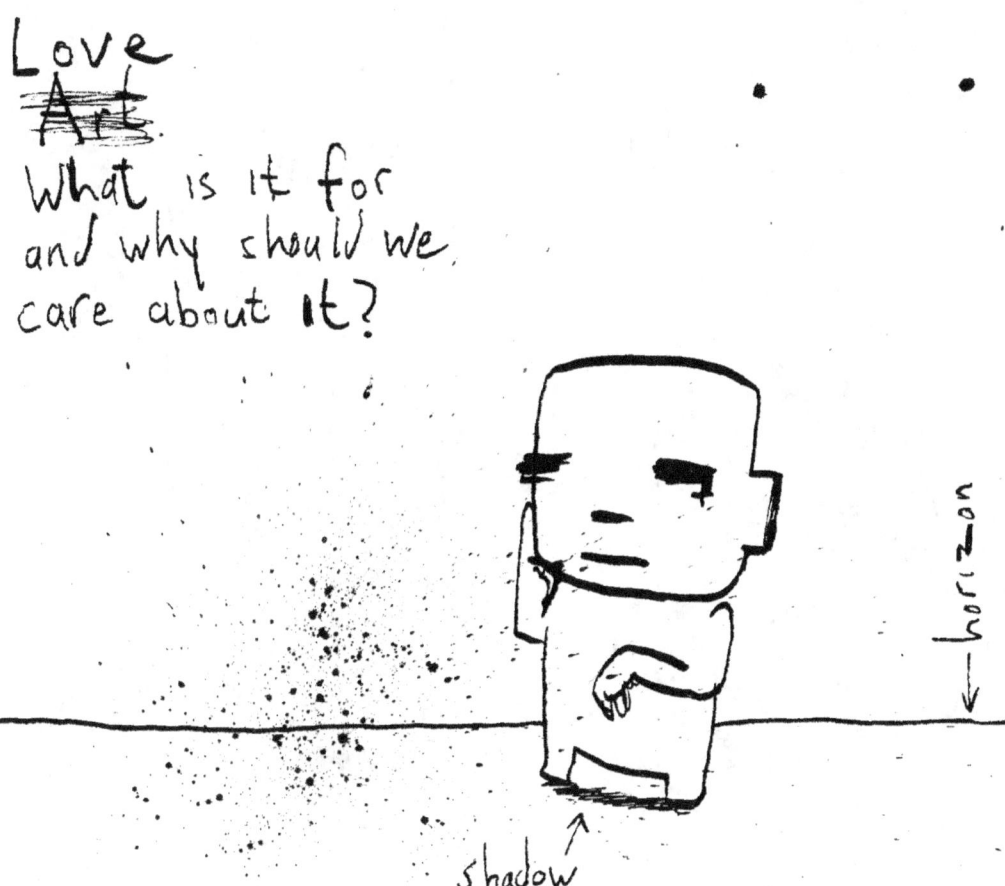

shadow

horizon

And on tuesdays

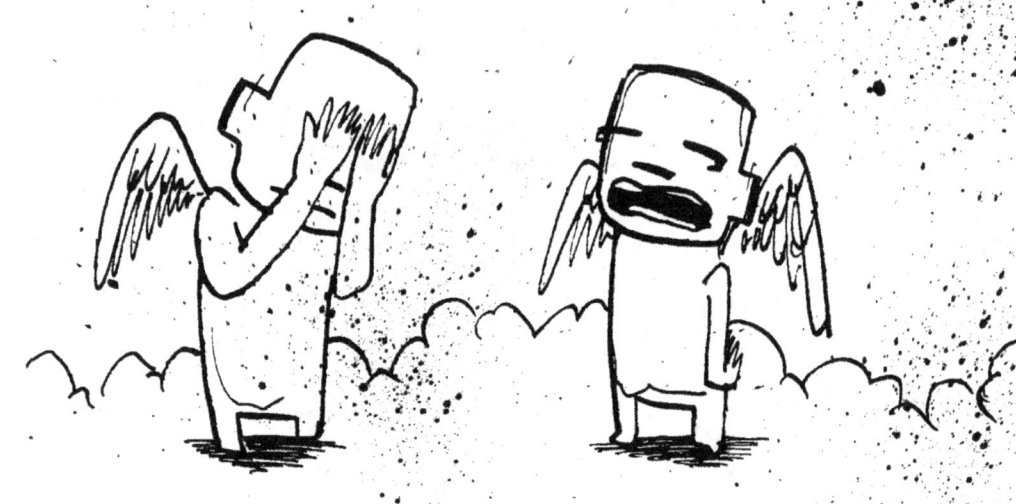

the angels wept

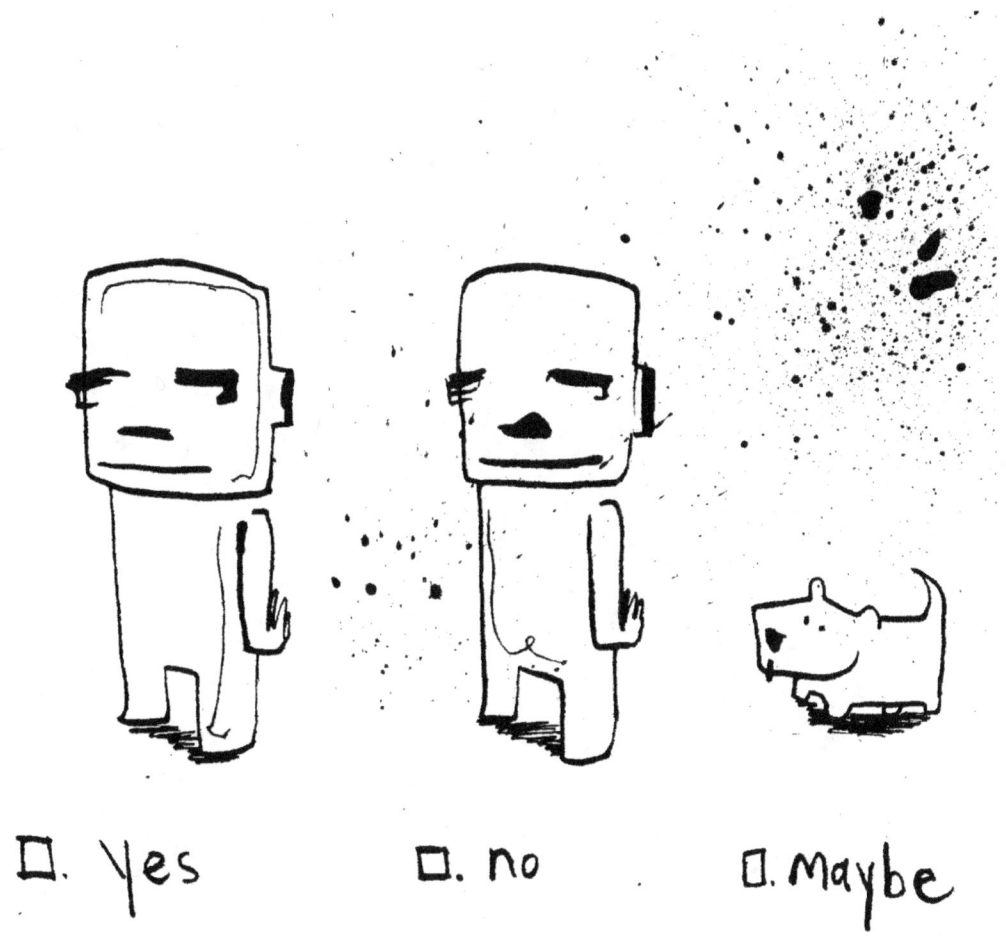

☐. yes   ☐. no   ☐.maybe

Part 3

About science and other forms
of reality.

What's really
inside a camel: ..

horizon →

sand dune ↓

shadow ↗

Chemistry Joke

proton

neutron

golf ball

Connect each child to
it's favorite pet.

1   2.   3

A   B   C

elephant   dog   leech

First we will
copy your brain
and store it on
computer chips

Later we will put the
chips in childrens toys.

one of these creatures
is not really a child.
Which one?

Answer: _ _ _ _

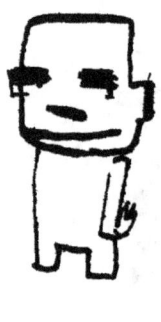

a.

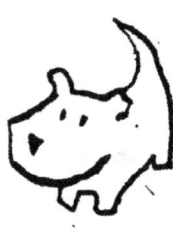

b.

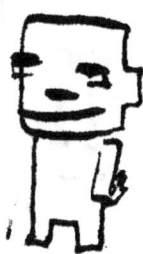

c.

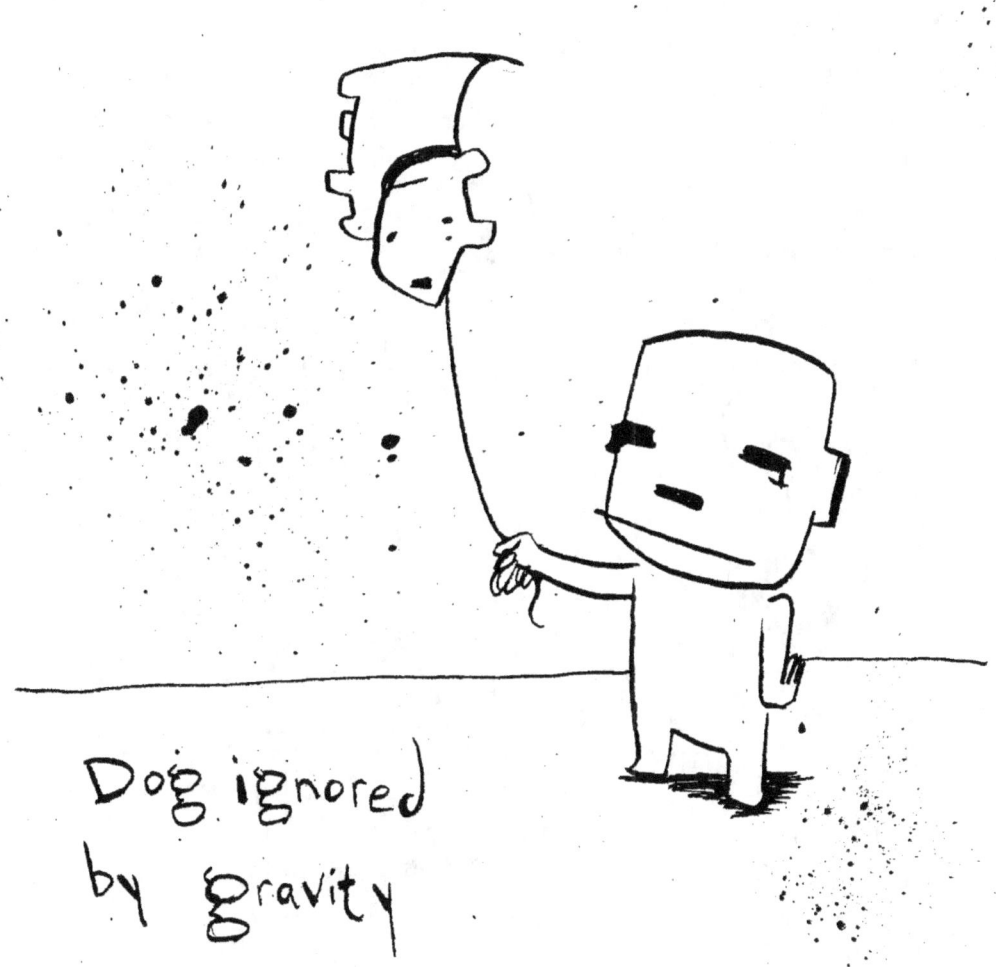

Dog ignored
by gravity

May 12, 2074;

Dogs will be dogs

cats will be
rabbits

No one knew what was
going on in her head

$\emptyset = 12,7912$

But even if
they did, it
would not
make any sense.

I.Q. test:

□. fear
□. sex
□. death
□. man sitting
   on a chair.

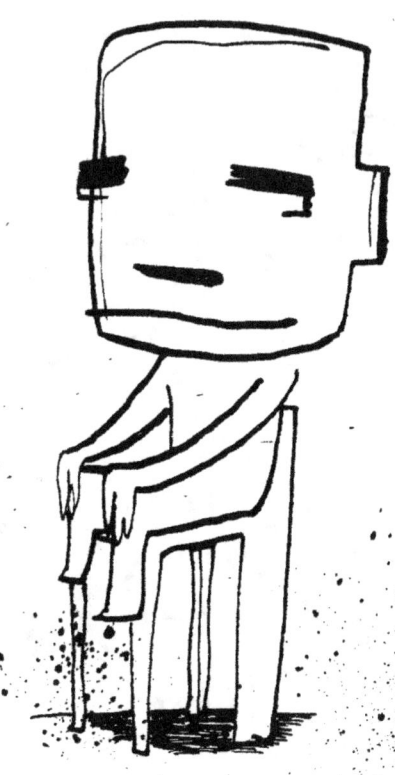

Meet James P. Murphy

The incredible human
shadow generator.

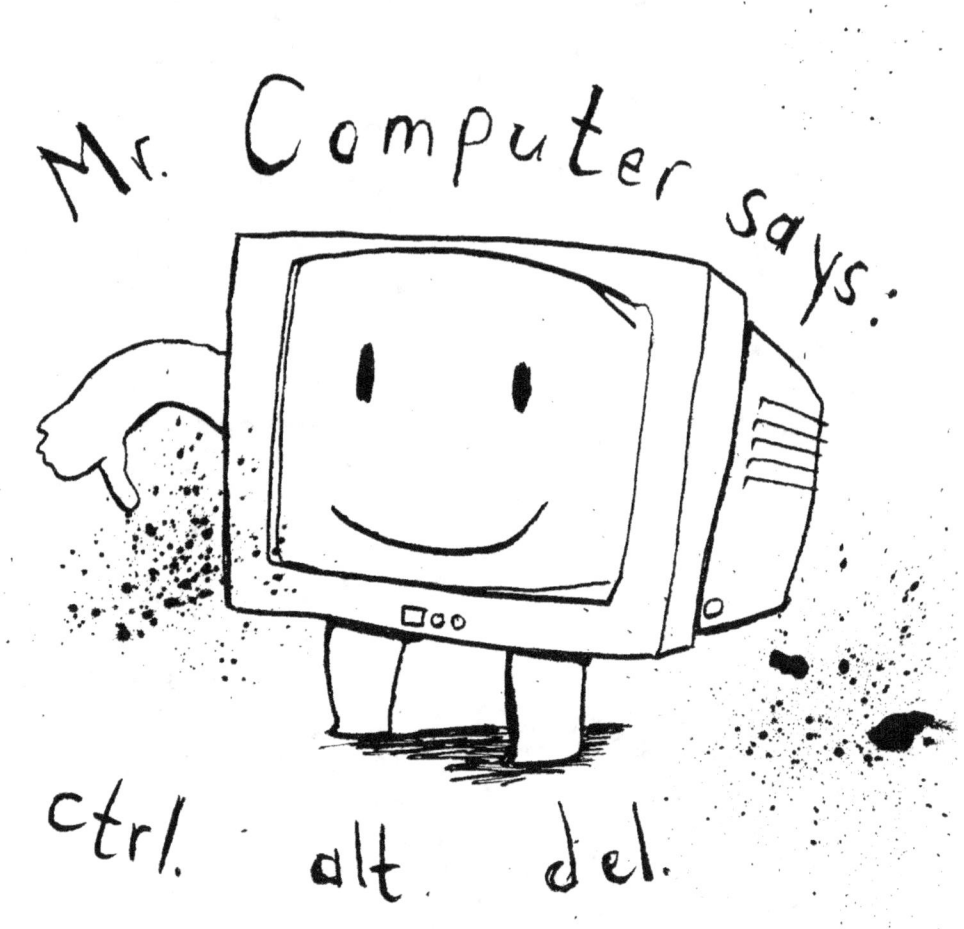

Mr. Computer says:

ctrl. alt. del.

optical illusion.

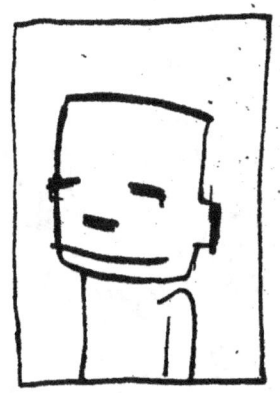 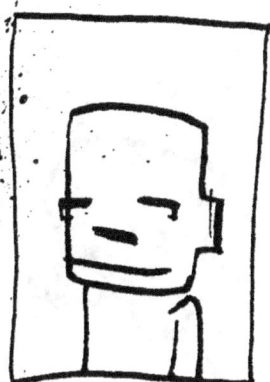

framed picture
of a man.

man behind
window.

I know, it is magical & creepy.

Never trust your eyes!

Unlike children,
roses weep in
silence.

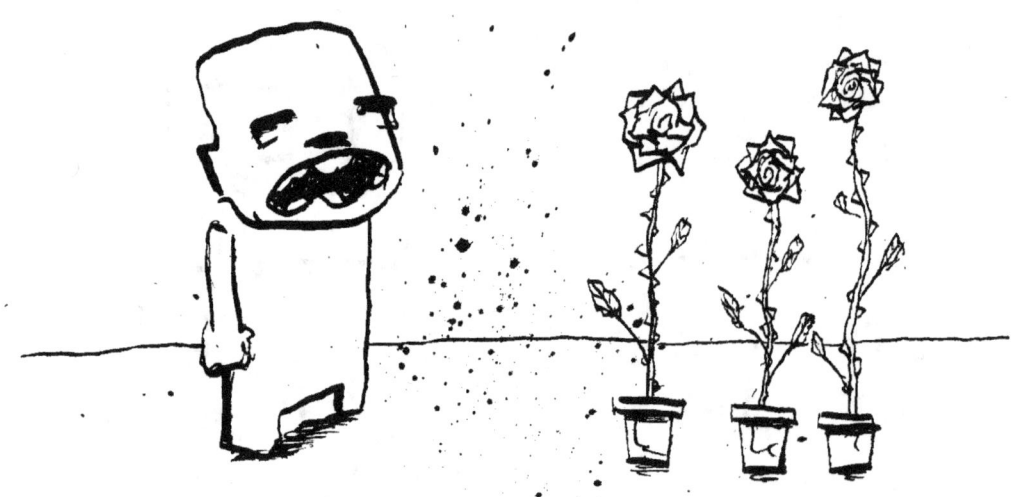

The difference between
snails and snakes:

They move in
opposite directions

They thought he was just
showing off, but his moped
had a flat tire

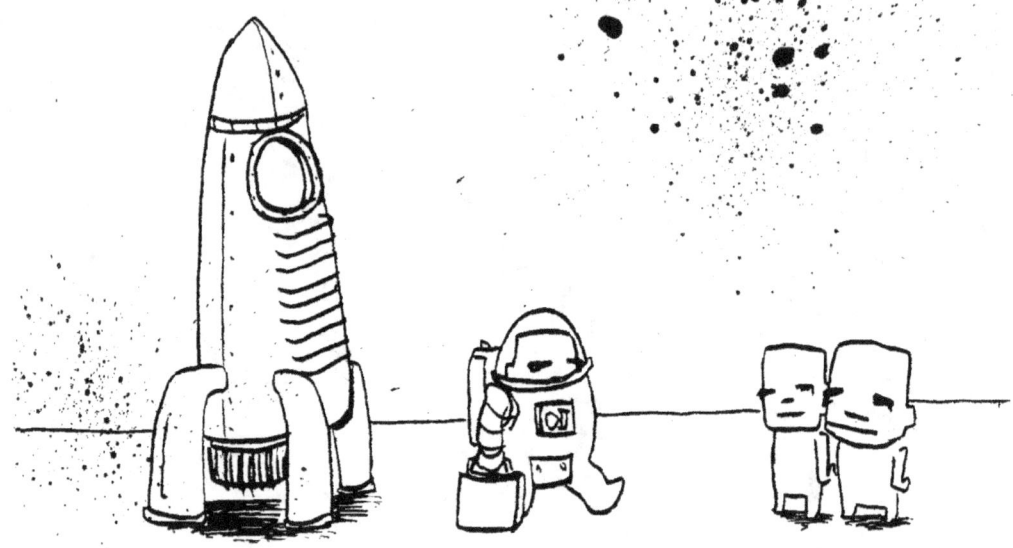

So the spaceman had to go to the
grocery store by rocket.

How to stay sane:

1. Plant the seed
2. Harvest the crop
3. Eat the crop
4. Return to phase 1

fig. 1a; the Human

oxygen →

food →

H₂O →

• water

→ Promises

→ bad ideas

→ secrets everybody already knows

Transitions

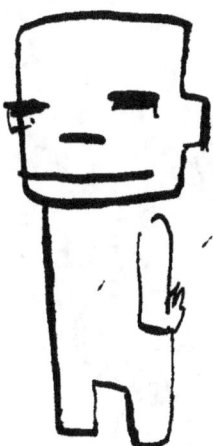 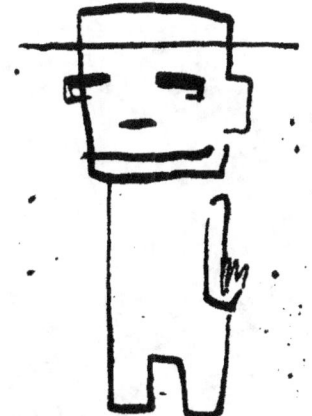

1a. kid   1b. kid with hat

This tree has
no penis

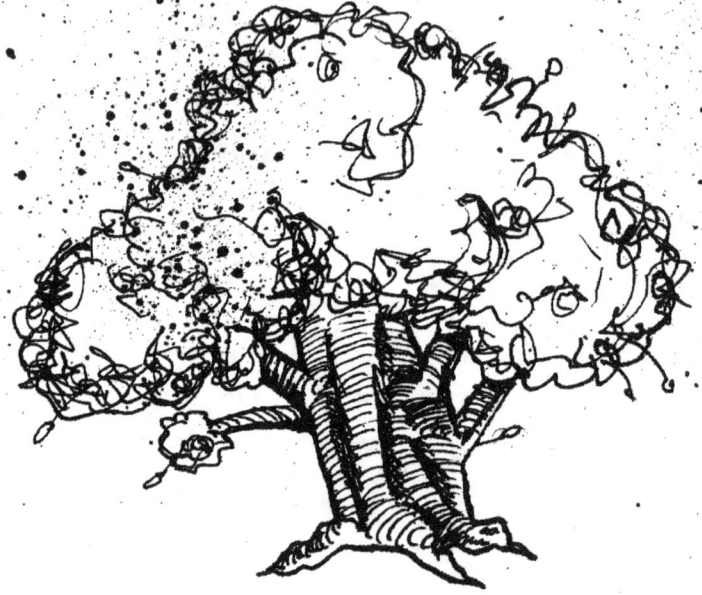

but that does not make it a woman .

Part 4

About the things that make your life
more or less successful.

This is the sword
Billy used to slay the
dragon

This is the fork
Billy used to eat
his potatoes

Billy is a remarkable man.

Before he became
a superhero

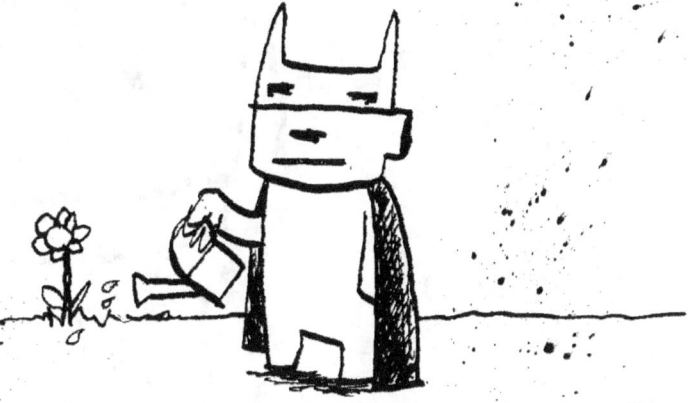

Batman was
a gardener.

Dance
like there will
be no tomorrow

Get drunk
like there was
no yesterday

Have sex
like you know
what you are doing

This is Fred.
Fred thinks
walking is for
the common man

horizon ←

Therefore
he floats.

← shadow

This Is where the fun is

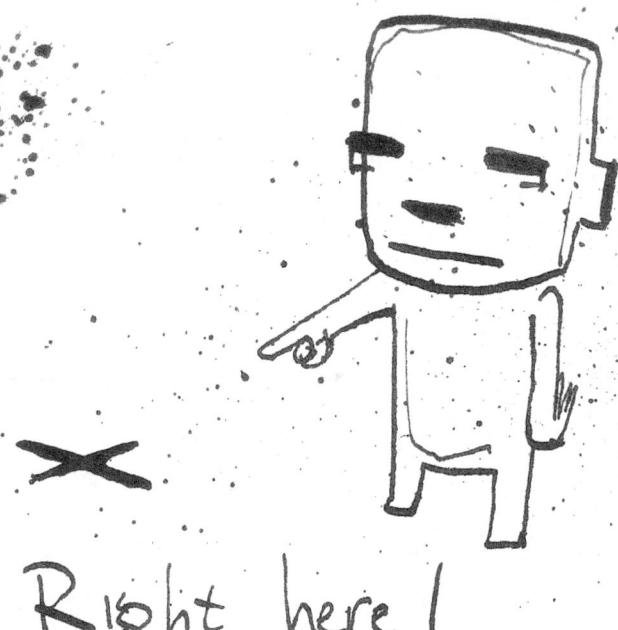

X

Right here!

This kid is not allowed.
to dance on the table

Soon his parents
will find out, because
the dog* will tell them.

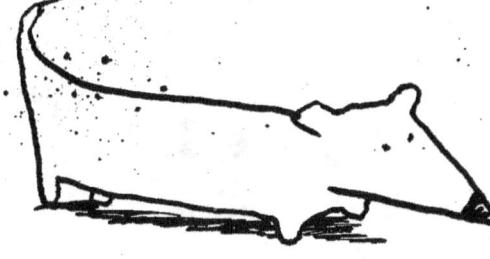

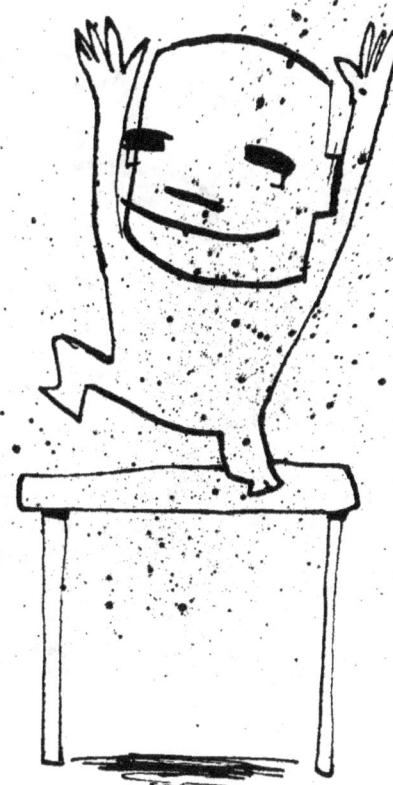

* it is german

It takes a Keen eye to spot the difference between modern dance and a catastrophe.

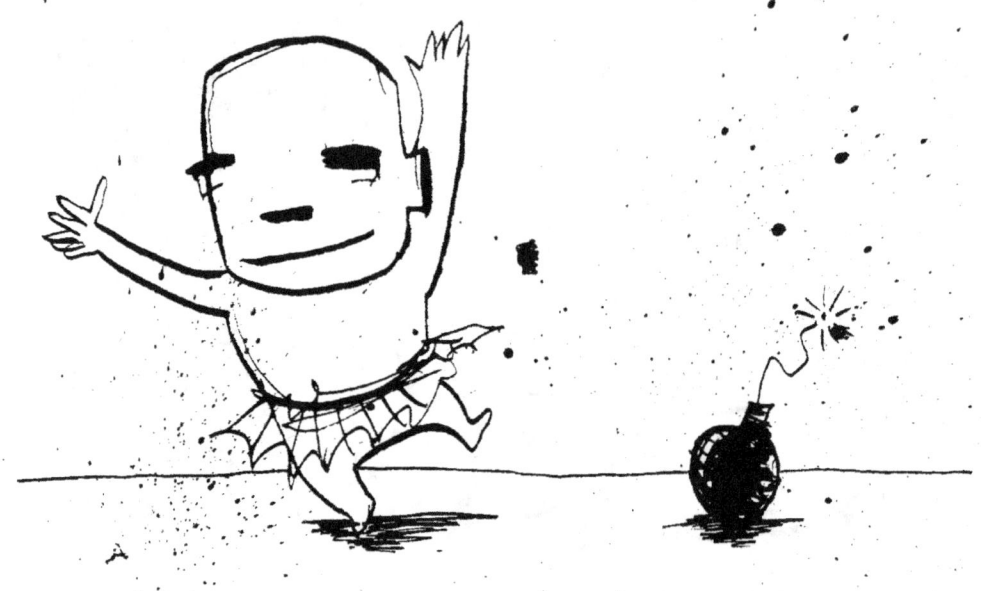

To lean against the wind

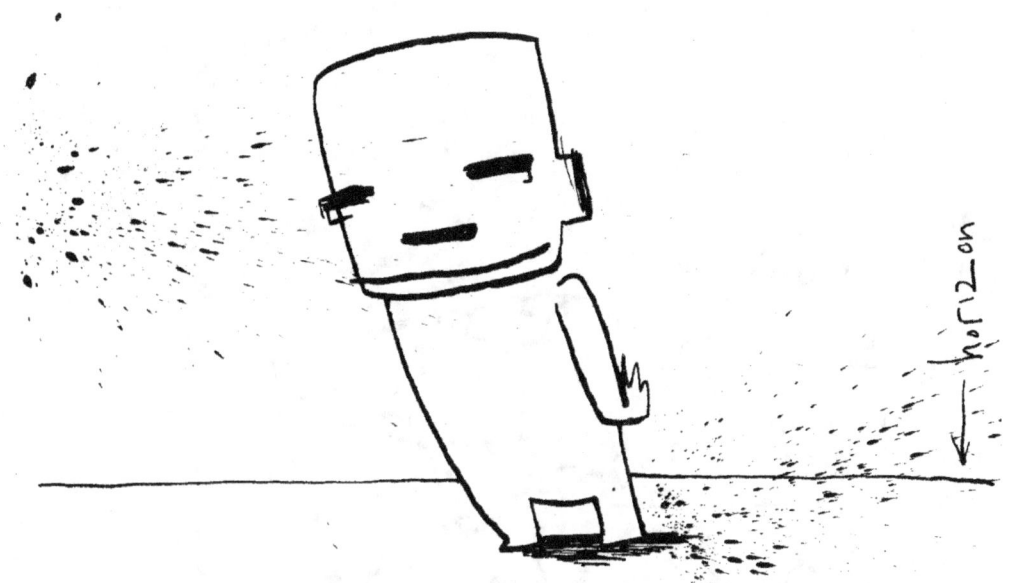

is to show you have plenty
of time for work.

When all goes wrong

Masturbation
is <u>always</u> an
option.

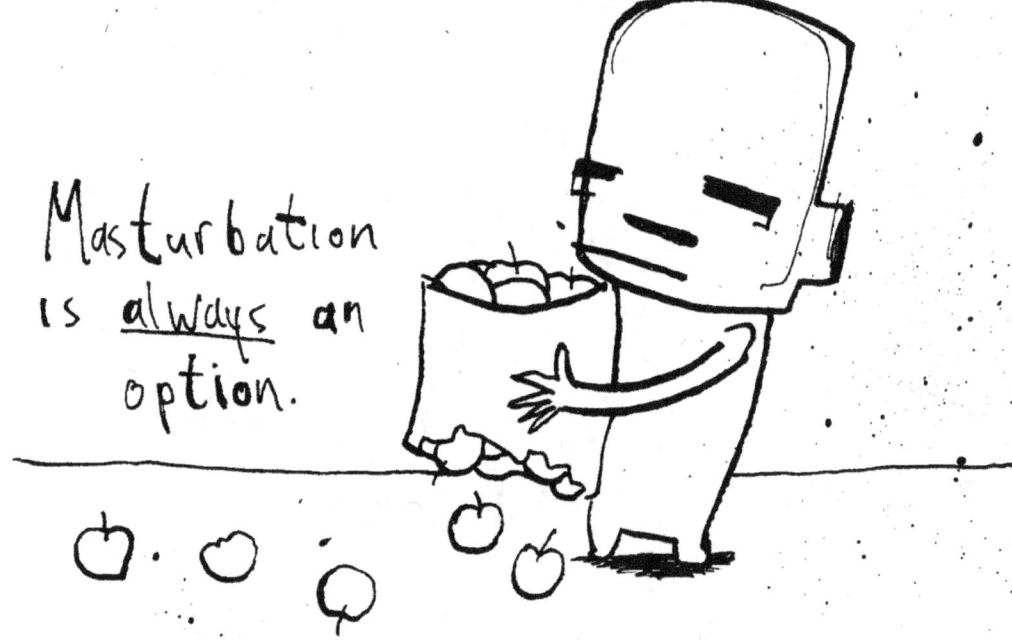

The monster hid under my parents bed, and scared the hell out of them.

This was hysterically funny

Never mind my.
hat.

Mind your
children.

(they are smoking
crack behind
the house)

Dance like a
common
~~MaD~~ MaN

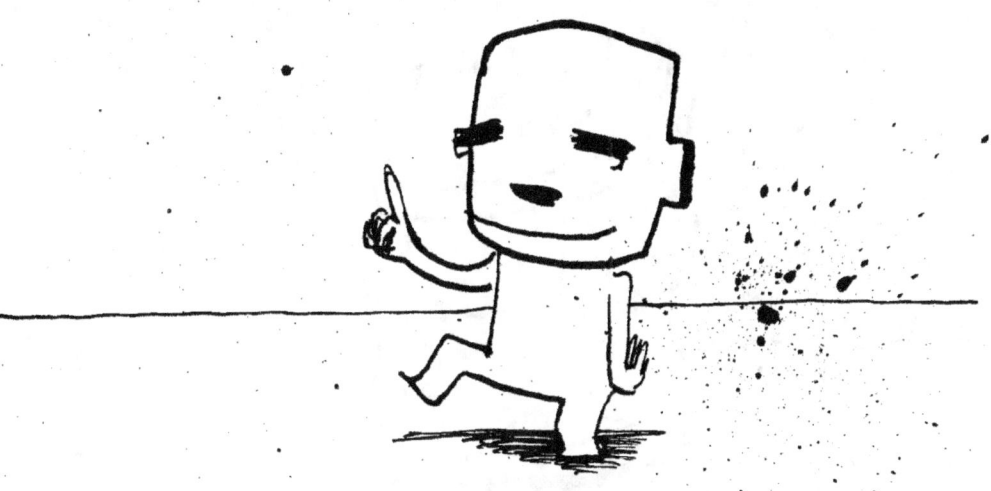

No is the new Yes.

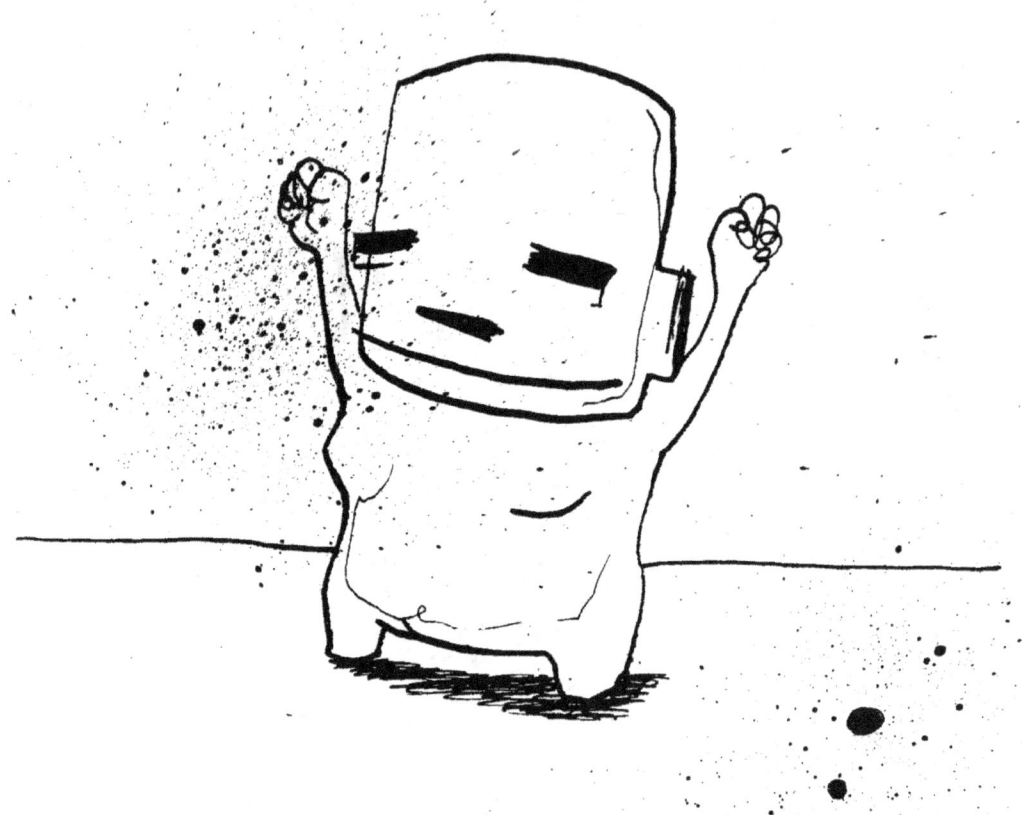

This is a dance.

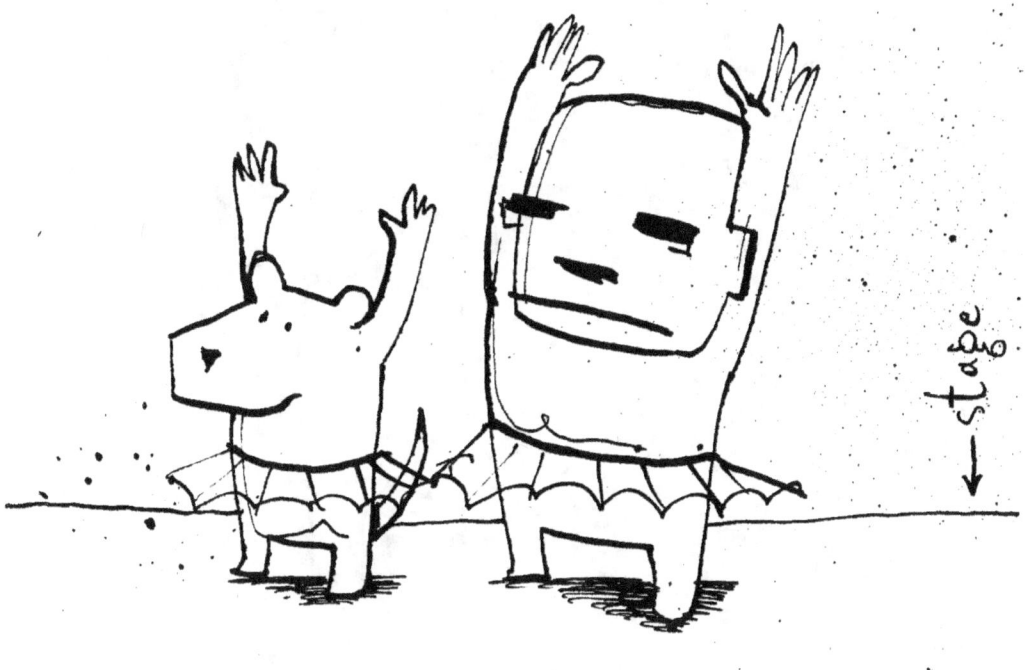

stage →

Not a robbery.

This is Peter

First he was
strong

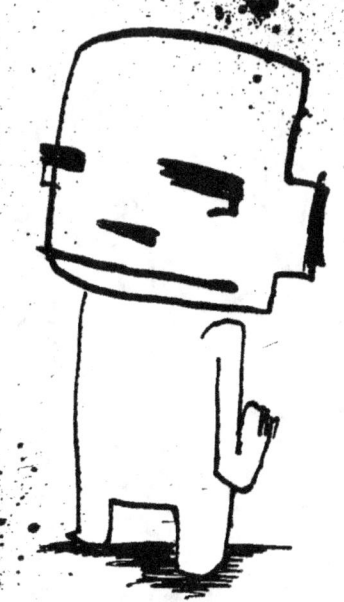

Then he
became weak

Now he is sort of
in between.

Revolution

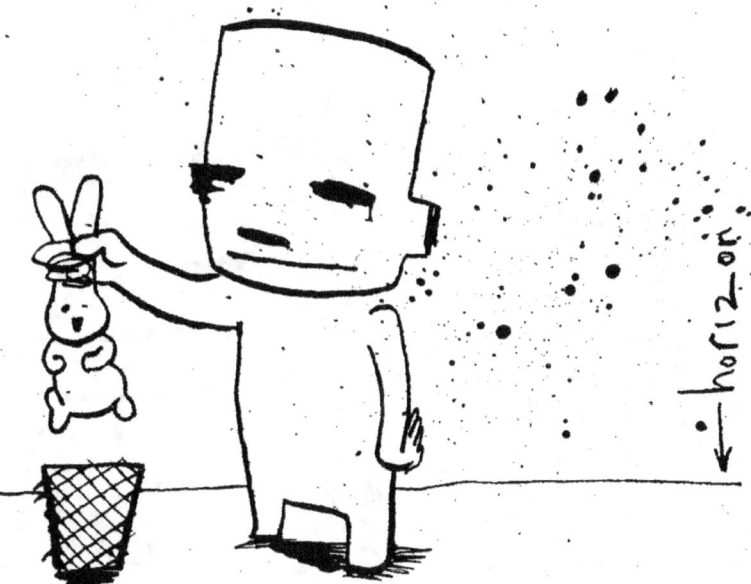

horizon ↓

The revolution started with a small gesture.

He who want's to be a Rockstar

must eat his Vegetables.

(fuck yeah).

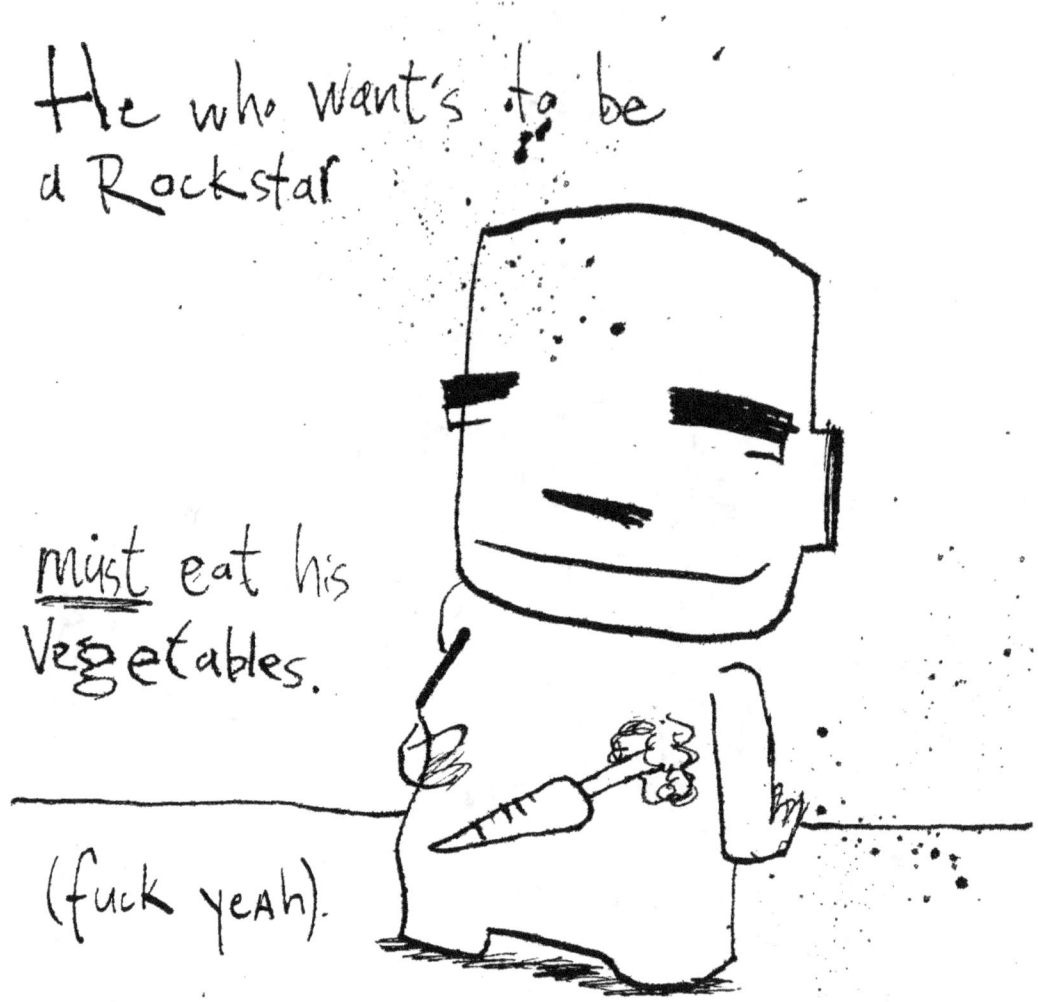

She
walked in
slow motion
because it
made her
look more
interesting

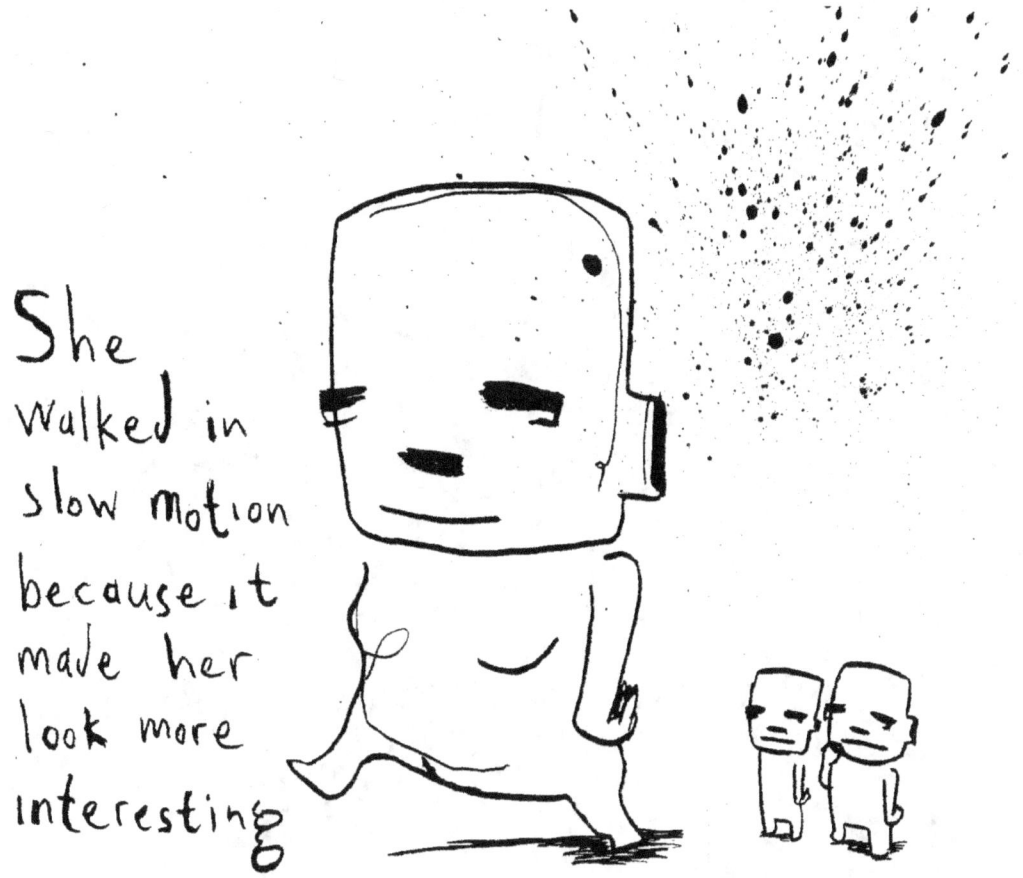

There is no "I"
in teamwork

but there are two
in Superstition.

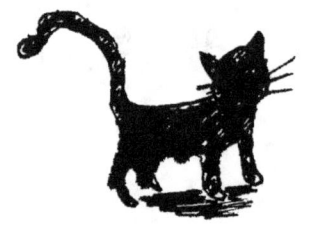

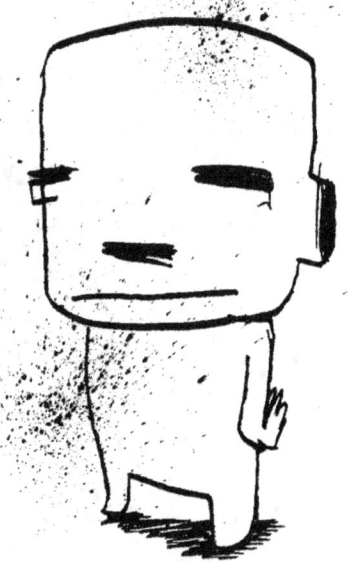

Does this help?

Hail to the teeth

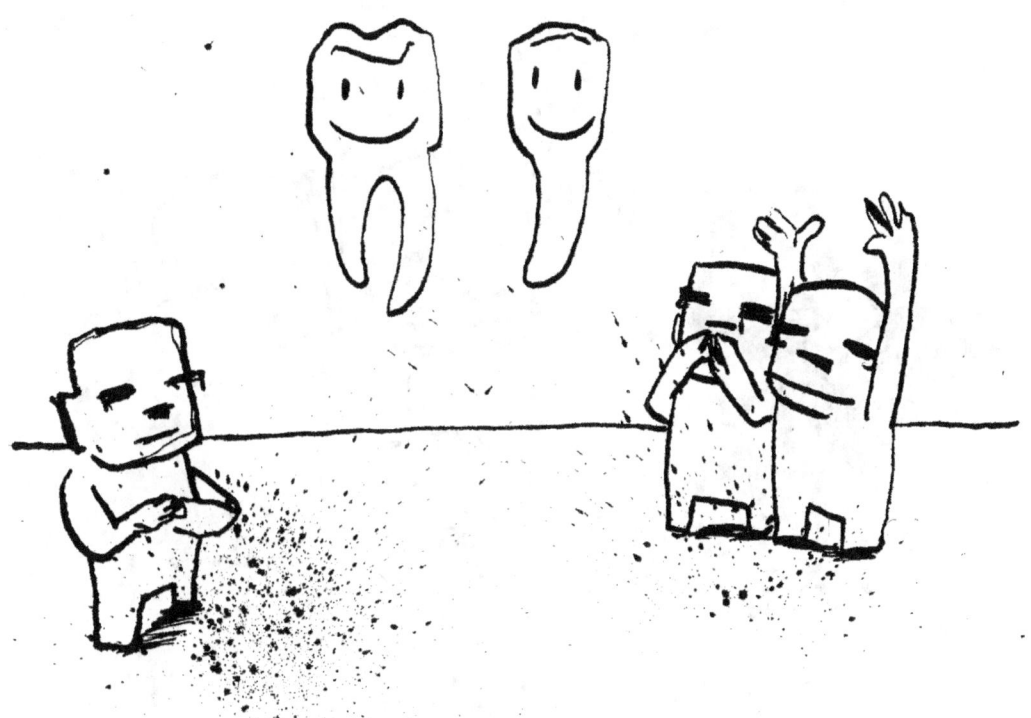

The wolf came and
took the children.

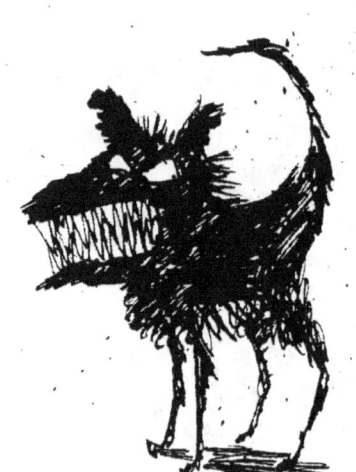 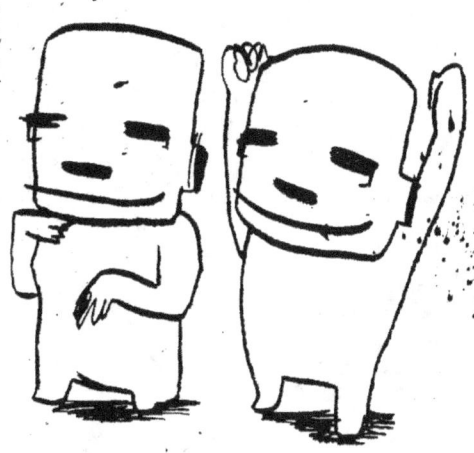

He left huge piles of cash,
and tickets to Disneyland.™

There is a very thin line

HUMAN

thin line

FRIDGE

between being a human, and
being something completely different.

Some dogs never
learn the truth

others are smart enough
to ignore it

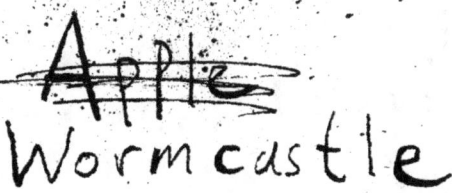

~~Apple~~ Wormcastle

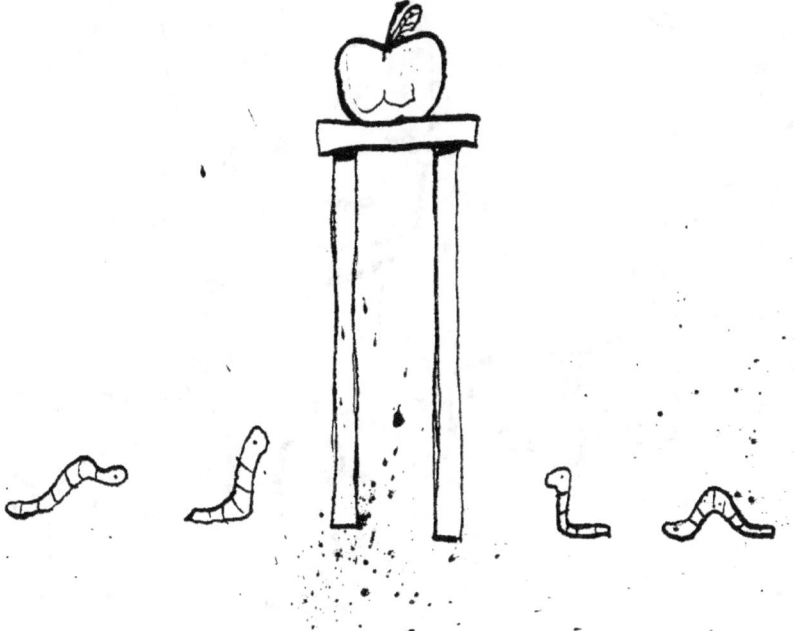

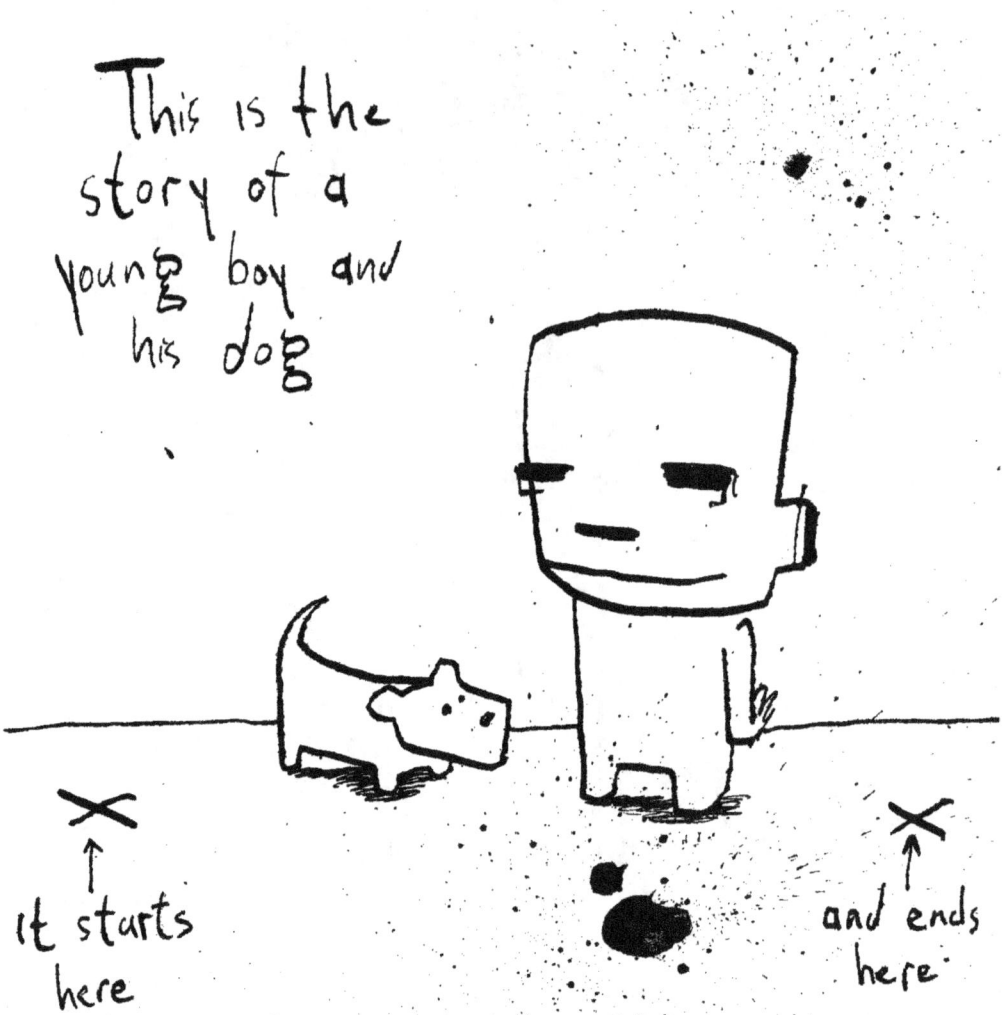

This is the
story of a
young boy and
his dog

It starts
here

and ends
here

This is the end of the book.
You may now go on with your life.

www.ingramcontent.com/pod-product-compliance
Lightning Source LLC
Chambersburg PA
CBHW082111220526
45472CB00009B/2131